Arafura

Timor Sea

DARWIN

Northern

Alice Springs

Western Australia

South

INDIAN OCEAN

PERTH (0/4125)
Northam (99/4026)
Kellerberrin (205/3920)
Carrabin (305/3820)
Yellowdine (4053720)
Coolgardie (559/3566)
Norseman (726/3399)
Balladonia (918/3207)
Caiguna (1100/3025)
Madura (1258/2867)
Mundrabilla (1375/2750)
Border Village (1453/2672)
Nullarbor (1639/2486)
Nundroo (1784/2...
Ced...

GREAT EASTERN HWY

Nullarbor Plain

EYRE HWY

Great Australian Bight

SOUTHERN

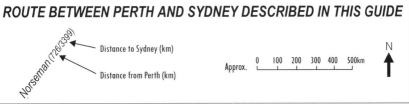

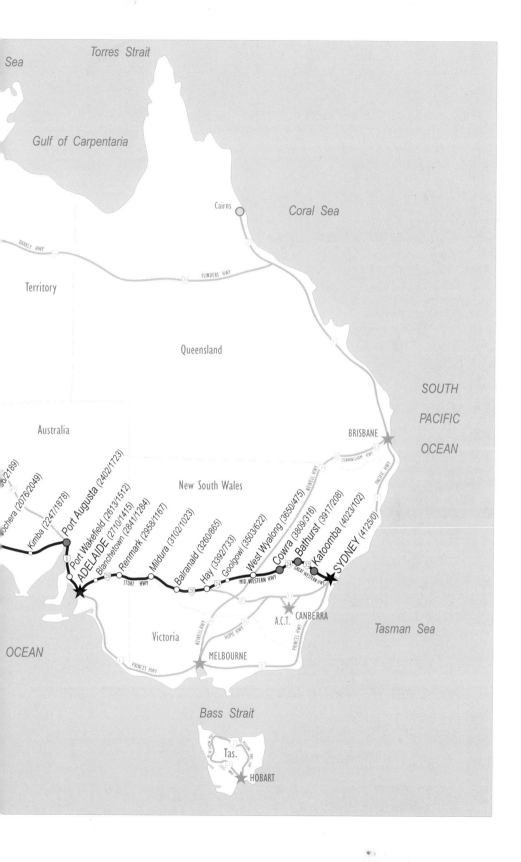

For Eileen

BIKE
AUSTRALIA
CYCLING AUSTRALIA FROM PERTH TO SYDNEY

Paul Salter

AN
EPIC
GUIDE

Epic Guides
PO Box 31053
Milford
New Zealand

www.epicguides.co.nz

1st Edition Published 2001
Copyright © Epic New Zealand Ltd, 2001
ISBN 0-9582256-0-5

Disclaimer and Safety Note:
The author and publisher do not accept responsibility for the safety or enjoyment of any person using this book or for any errors or omissions. No guide can identify the limitations of every reader, or all the potential hazards on a journey; check conditions before setting out and use common sense on your trip.

INTRODUCTION

Imagine cycling the longest straight sealed road in the world, crossing a huge limestone plain below a brilliant blue sky, the horizon encircling and the nearest outpost of civilisation over 90km away - Australia is a great place to cycle tour!

Australia's vast expanses, sun soaked climate, and undeveloped Outback areas draw long distance bicycle tourers, but they also present significant challenges. Because of the large distances between some towns and the often harsh climate, Australia is not the place to undertake your first extended bicycle tour. But, for those with a good level of fitness and some bike touring experience, this is one of the great cycling frontiers.

This guidebook describes the ultimate Trans-Australian cycle journey; eastward 4200km from Perth in Western Australia, to the country's biggest city Sydney in New South Wales, crossing the continent from the Indian Ocean to the Pacific. The tour is a direct route across the country that follows main roads. It passes through remote wilderness areas, Australia's rural heartland, and the cities of Perth, Adelaide, and Sydney - a total of four of Australia's six states. A highlight of the trip is crossing the Nullarbor Plain, a vast expanse, beautiful in its own isolated and sparse way. For 1,200km along this section there is little evidence of human activity apart from the road and the tiny roadhouses dotted along the way.

The aim of this guide is to provide cycle tourers with the information needed to undertake part, or all, of this tour, and to give some background on the sites along the way. It also includes a unique photographic record of the route: at 100km intervals between Perth and Sydney photographs give an idea of the terrain and road conditions that can be expected across Australia.

The guide is split into two parts. Part I deals with Getting To Australia, When To Come, and What To Bring. Once you're in Australia it includes information on Where To Stay, Internal Travel, and how to get by in the Aussie Culture. The On The Road section explains what to expect when cycle touring on Australian roads.

Part II describes the journey between Perth and Sydney. The route is divided into 30 stages ranging in length from 78km to 211km. Each stage is presented on 2 pages of the guide, as shown on page 30. These stages can be tackled in a day, or split, depending on riding conditions and individual fitness. Intermediate stops are listed, however several long stages have no intermediate stops and, unless they can be covered in a day, will require unsupported camping. Food, water, camping facilities and accommodation are available at the end of each stage and a selection of campground, hostel, hotel and motel accommodation is provided. Details on bicycle shops and tourist information centres along the way are also included.

Strip maps show the route and profile for each stage, and a general description of the cycling terrain is given in the text. Individual hills are not listed. Town and city maps have been included for places that you might consider spending rest days in, along with a description of some of the sites in these towns. Part II also includes possible alternative routes for those looking for even more kilometres, although these are not described in detail in this guide.

Australia is a metric country so all distances given are in kilometres. Prices are quoted in Australian dollars. For those who don't favour cycling long distances between remote towns, consider doing part of this tour in the more populated east; Adelaide to Sydney via the Murray River towns for example, or, if you hanker for the real Outback of Australia's desert centre, take one of the guided tours described in Part I which offer bike trips with most of the details arranged.

Whatever you choose - enjoy cycling Australia.

TABLE OF CONTENTS

PART I - PREPARATIONS

ON THE ROAD

PART II – THE JOURNEY

WESTERN AUSTRALIA

SOUTH AUSTRALIA

PART I
PREPARATIONS

GETTING TO AUSTRALIA

Airlines and Bringing a Bike to Australia

Most major airlines fly to Australia. Many fly non-stop to Sydney and some fly directly to Perth. Your choice of airline will depend on your departure point, any desired stopovers, and probably high on your list - price. Shop around for good fares to Australia and check for any hidden costs associated with bringing your bicycle. An Australian departure tax of $27 is automatically included in your ticket price. You may want to limit the number of connecting flights due to the hassle of collecting and re-checking your bike gear mid-trip.

You can bring your bicycle on your flight as personal luggage; however, your total baggage must still be within the airlines weight allowance. Most airlines require a bicycle to be bagged or boxed, with the tires deflated. Some airlines will allow your bike to be loaded unboxed with the pedals removed or turned inwards, the handlebars turned sideways, and the chain covered. Cardboard bike boxes can be obtained from bicycle shops which usually throw them away (don't do business with a shop that tries to make you pay for one). Pack your touring gear in plastic bags around your bike to protect it in the box. Some airlines will treat a bike as an item of baggage at no extra charge; others charge a significant fee for bikes. Be sure to check when booking your flights.

Entry Requirements

To enter Australia you'll need a passport and a visa. Your home country issues passports and there's usually a cost associated. Keep your passport with you at all times. It's your most important travel document and losing it could mean an extended stay until your Embassy, Consulate, or High Commission can re-issue you a new one. You should carry a separate photocopy of your passport, and leave another copy at home. The passport should be valid for the length of your stay in Australia and at least three months beyond.

A visa gives you permission to enter the country for a certain period. An Australian visa must be obtained at home before coming to Australia (New Zealanders are an exception - they can get their visa on arrival). To obtain a visa complete an application form and submit it, along with your passport, to an Australian diplomatic office in your home country. Another method, recently introduced, for getting a visa is the ETA (Electronic Travel Authority) system. This system allows airlines and travel agents to obtain authorisation for you to enter Australia at the same time they book your flights via their computer network. The ETA system currently operates in 31 countries (including the UK, most EC countries, USA, Canada, and Japan), so check when booking flights to see if this is an option.

An Australian tourist visa lets you stay in the country for up to three months at a time and is valid for one year. You can apply for a longer stay, either before you leave home (a fee is involved) or in Australia before your 3 months expires (a larger fee is involved). It is illegal to work on a tourist visa.

Immigration regulations change from time to time so check visa and entry requirements before leaving home. If you arrive without a valid visa you're liable to be put on the next plane home. The Australian Government maintains an Internet site *(www.immi.gov.au)* with visa information and the overseas locations of Australia's diplomatic offices.

Customs

Like most Western countries Australia has strict laws on the importation of firearms, weapons, explosive or flammable goods, narcotics, live animals, products made from

60 million years ago Australia breaks from Antarctica and becomes its own continent

endangered species, organic goods and food items. You can't bring in more than A$5,000 cash or equivalent currency either. Also, ensure your tent and bicycle tires are free of dirt to avoid complications with customs clearance. Keep in mind your home country's duty regulations when returning with purchases made in Australia.

Health

No special health precautions are needed before coming to Australia. However, if in the previous two weeks you visited a country that is known for yellow fever, small-pox, cholera, or typhoid you must obtain an International Certificate of Vaccination before entering Australia.

The quality of tap water in Australia is good (although a giardia and cryptosporidium outbreak did occur in Sydney a few years back). Stream and river water may be affected by giardia and should be treated before use.

The mosquito-borne viruses, Ross River fever, Barmah Forest disease, and Murray Valley encephalitis are present in some rural areas and precautions should be taken to avoid getting bitten.

The Australian sun is fierce. Aussie's have the world's highest incidence of skin cancer, so take plenty of sunscreen and reapply it often. Loose light clothing also provides protection from the sun. Be conscious of dehydration when cycling in the heat. Drink water frequently, starting early in the day and before you feel thirsty, and cycle with a steady rhythm avoiding bouts of extreme exertion. *See also Hazards, p.28*

Insurance

Travel insurance is worth having. Comprehensive policies cover medical expenses, airline cancellations, and loss of luggage. Some credit card companies offer free limited insurance if you use their card to book travel. Unless you are a New Zealander, you're not covered by Australia's health care system and you'll be responsible for any medical costs incurred.

Discounts

Student ID, ISIC, Youth Hostel Association (YHA) and other backpacker ID cards can sometimes get you travel and accommodation discounts. Automobile Club memberships may also earn you discounts on car rentals and accommodation.

WHEN TO CYCLE TOUR

Summer is not the time to undertake this journey. Inland temperatures during the summer months (December through February) can be fearsome, often exceeding 40°C (104°F), and on the Nullarbor, winds from the east are common. Spring (September through November) and autumn (March through May) are good times to cycle from Perth to Sydney, although March can still get very hot. Spring in particular is a good time to bike in Western Australia; the state's wildflowers are at their best and afternoon winds from the west predominate. Winter (June to August) can be okay for bicycle touring too, although be prepared for bitterly cold nights and frequent rain.

Travelling between Perth and Sydney in spring and autumn you can expect mostly sunny days with warm to hot temperatures. Nights are cool to cold. Expect some showers, although it can rain for days on end anywhere along the route so be prepared. Average temperature and rainfall data for selected towns between Perth and Sydney are included in Appendix A. There are about 12 hours of daylight between sunrise and sunset in springtime.

In other parts of Australia the weather varies widely. In the tropical north it's almost always hot, with a dry season roughly from April to October and a wet season for the rest of the year. In the south during winter, snow falls on the highlands of Victoria and southern New South Wales, and Tasmania is cold and wet.

December and January are the busiest tourist times in Australia. During holiday periods it can also be more difficult to book accommodation and travel *(see p.24 for holiday dates)*. During January, when families often take holidays together, some businesses operate with skeleton staff.

WHAT TO TAKE

Plan to take the minimum gear you'll need to cover the worst anticipated conditions, then add just enough to be able to live from day to day. Travelling as light as possible avoids over-stressing you and your bike, and allows you to cover a decent distance in a day. The route is sealed all the way, and tourers have undertaken this trip on road bikes (generally with triple chain rings and touring tires), mountain bikes (slick tires are a help) and hybrid touring bikes. The bike you use should be a good fit, have sufficient load carrying capacity, and have a reasonably lightweight frame with good quality components. Needless to say, it has to be in 100% working order.

The long unsupported distances on this tour mean you should be prepared to camp out and have enough tools and know-how to repair your bike if it breaks down.

A rainjacket is the most important item of clothing, for fighting wind chill in the early mornings and for inclement weather. It should be made of a waterproof and breathable fabric. A light- to mid-weight fleece top is the second most important piece of clothing. With a good rainjacket and warm top you should be able to survive a cold wet night almost anywhere. Lightweight polypropylene longs, and a polypropylene top with a long zip, allow you to dress in layers and control your temperature. Lightweight rain pants, over gloves and shoe covers are worth having, but will probably spend most of their time in the bottom of a pannier. For the midday heat, bike shorts and a bike shirt (or T-shirt) are generally sufficient. You'll want to pack plenty of sunscreen for use on any exposed skin, and long sleeves and a collar will also protect you from the sun. Wrap-around sunglasses provide protection from windblown grit and dust. A helmet is a legal requirement for cycling in Australia.

You could consider taking a tent fly, poles, and a light plastic ground sheet rather than a full tent in order to save weight. A small down sleeping bag and an Ultralight 3/4 Thermarest® pad are ideal. It's possible to leave cooking equipment behind too and plan cold meals, which can be supplemented with hot food bought along way. The following is a suggested gear list that should pack into rear panniers, on the top of a rear rack, and in a handlebar bag.

BIKE
Bike with racks.. ☐
Panniers and handlebar bag.. ☐
Water bottles and cages.. ☐
Cycle computer... ☐
Small flashing LCD rear light.. ☐

CAMPING
Tent (or tent fly, poles, and ground sheet).................................... ☐
Sleeping bag and mat... ☐

1606 The Dutchman Willem Jansz sights the northern coast of Australia while exploring for gold in New Guinea

Small towel... ☐
Small torch (flashlight)... ☐
Plate and spoon... ☐
Toilet paper... ☐

CLOTHING
Rainjacket... ☐
Lightweight rain pants.. ☐
Light- to mid-weight fleece top... ☐
Polypropylene underwear (top and longs), hat, and gloves............ ☐
2 T-shirts or cycle tops.. ☐
1 Pair of lightweight shorts... ☐
1 or 2 Pairs of sox.. ☐
1 or 2 Pairs of underwear.. ☐
1 Pair of lightweight longs.. ☐
1 or 2 Pairs of cycle shorts... ☐
Cycle gloves.. ☐
1 Pair of shoes... ☐
Sunglasses... ☐
Reflector sash.. ☐
Bicycle helmet... ☐

TOOLS
Pump, puncture repair kit, tire levers.. ☐
Spare inner tube... ☐
Tire patch or spare tire... ☐
Spare spokes (including spokes for the rear cluster side) and spoke wrench...... ☐
Cluster removing tool.. ☐
Chain breaker.. ☐
Spare brake and gear cables.. ☐
Spare nuts and bolts (including rack bolts)................................... ☐
Appropriate allen keys.. ☐
Wrench, pliers, screw driver.. ☐
Zip ties, some duct tape, grease & lube, small rag......................... ☐

MISCELLANEOUS
Bike lock.. ☐
Pocket knife with tin opener... ☐
Small First-Aid kit and sewing kit.. ☐
Plastic bags to wrap gear in wet weather..................................... ☐
Matches and candle.. ☐
Camera and film... ☐
Toiletries and medications (including sunscreen and insect repellent)........... ☐
Maps, small compass, personal documents.................................... ☐
Emergency water bottle, water purification tablets or pump............. ☐

OPTIONAL EXTRAS
Stove, fuel, pot.. ☐
Rear view mirror.. ☐
Hydration backpack.. ☐

IN AUSTRALIA

Crash Course in Australian History

Australia has always been a unique place. Even before humans arrived, the continent had its own special flora and fauna due in part to its isolation from other landmasses. The first people to walk the land were Aboriginal, probably arriving by canoe, from Southeast Asia over 50,000 years ago. It's estimated there where at least 500,000 Aborigines in Australia, living a semi-nomadic tribal lifestyle with complex customs and rituals, at the time of European settlement.

Europe's philosophers and geographers had guessed at the existence of a Great South Land - Terra Australis - which they thought must exist to balance the landmasses of the Northern Hemisphere. But it was the Dutch during their explorations of the East Indies (Indonesia) who were the first Europeans to actually sight Australia in 1606. Although exploratory voyages followed, the Dutch East India Co. thought the land looked unprofitable and never established an outpost. The British explorer Cook discovered Australia's eastern coast in 1770, claimed it for George III, and gave it the name New South Wales. Cook very nearly lost his ship in Australia when he ran aground on a reef. Luckily, as the ship was pulled off, a lump of coral broke off and plugged the hull.

On the strength of Cook's reports the First Fleet, about 1,500 people on 11 ships, set sail from Portsmouth in 1787 to establish a colony on the southern land. Over half the new arrivals were prisoners transported from over-crowded British prisons. After struggling, and nearly starving in this new land, the colony started to grow from its Sydney Cove base. Tasmania and Port Philip (Victoria) were settled, and in 1813 the vast interior started opening up after a route across the seemingly impenetrable Blue Mountains was discovered. The nineteenth century saw explorers set out in every direction across the continent (some never to be heard from again). The grazing lands, and then the gold, they discovered resulted in the growth of an agricultural and mineral based economy - sectors that continue to be the financial backbone of the country. In 1858 the population reached an estimated 1,000,000 and continued to grow despite an exodus to the Californian goldfields in the 1850's and a financial crisis in 1890's.

In 1901 the six colonies were united into the Commonwealth of Australia, governed from Melbourne by a British styled Parliament. Seven years later Canberra was chosen as the site for the capital in order to stem the rivalry between Sydney and Melbourne. The early part of the Twentieth Century was grim, with Australia participating in two world wars separated by the Great Depression. The ill-fated Gallipoli landings of World War I, where thousands of Australian and New Zealand soldiers died, are remembered each year on Anzac Day. During World War II Japanese expansion in the Pacific reached within a few hundred kilometres of Australia and Darwin was bombed before the tide turned. Sport became a diversion during the hard times of the Depression and Australians excelled on the world stage in swimming (Claire Dennis), tennis (Jack Crawford), horse racing (Phar Lap), and in epic cricket battles with the English (Don Bradman et. al.). The tough times during the first half of the Twentieth Century cemented Australia's national identity and laid the foundation for prosperity over the next 50 years.

Following World War II, migration to Australia increased greatly, with the vast majority coming from Britain and post-war Europe (the Government's infamous "White Australia" policies making it difficult for anyone else to come to Australia). The 1950's and 60's saw considerable economic development, with projects like the huge Snowy Mountains Hydroelectric Scheme. There was a general burgeoning of affluence that placed Australia second only to America in standard of living. However, the rosy picture

1627 A Dutch ship explores the southern coast of "New Holland" (Australia)

had blemishes. Aborigines were not considered citizens and could not vote until 1962.

In the 1970's Australia was shaken out of its complacency by an oil-fuelled world recession, which brought inflation and unemployment, and by a political crisis that resulted in the Government controversially being dismissed by the Queen's representative; The Governor-General.

During the 1980's the economy fluctuated and the Government moved towards free market policies and an alignment with Asia in an effort to bring growth. On the sporting scene Australia's sailors became national heroes in 1983 when, with the help of a secret winged keel, they became the first nation to beat the US for the world's oldest sporting trophy - the America's Cup. Australian-made feature films made an increasing impact on world screens in the 1980's and 1990's, with movies like "The Man from Snowy River", "Strictly Ballroom", and "Shine". In 1988 the Bicentennial Commemorations celebrated 200 years of European settlement.

The final decade of last century saw a gradual move to recognise Aboriginal land rights, an awareness of the political importance of environmental issues, and a vigorous debate over a possible Australian Republic. The stereotype of a land full of Outback bushmen had taken a hard knock by the end of the century; 80 percent of Australians lived in large cities with many never seeing the real Outback, but there was, and still is, a strong affinity many Australians feel towards the bush.

Australia is still a unique place - a melting pot of people in a strange, harsh, and beautiful land.

Note: Australia's six states and two capital territories are often abbreviated as follows; ACT = Australian Capital Territories, NSW = New South Wales, Qld. = Queensland, NT = Northern Territory, SA = South Australia, Tas. = Tasmania, Vic. = Victoria, WA = Western Australia. Australia also has several offshore territories and possessions.

ACCOMMODATION

Accommodation in Australia is generally of a good standard, although some of the places in smaller towns along this route, particularly in WA, are pretty basic. This guide provides a selection of accommodations along the route, although inclusion is not necessarily a recommendation. The rates listed are approximate - check when booking. During holiday periods it is best to book in advance for popular tourist towns. In remote areas you may want to check ahead that lodging is still offered.

Hotels and Motels
Hotels range from the budget to the luxury. Hotel rooms usually have tea and coffee making facilities and a private bathroom. Be aware that a hotel, especially in smaller towns, will often mean a public bar with accommodation upstairs. Motel rooms generally have cooking facilities for self-catering, refrigerators, tea and coffee facilities, and a private bathroom. Brand-name hotel and motel chains are present across the country, and their regional offices can supply location lists. In small towns independently run hotels and motels are more common.

Roadhouses are found in many remote areas. These are basically one-shop stops, typically providing petrol (gas), food, water, and basic motel or cabin accommodation. They generally have areas available for camping as well.

Hostels
Australia has a good network of hostels. The Youth Hostel Association has about 140 throughout the country, and there are many more independent hostels. Hostels provide

dormitory and sometimes private rooms, shared bathroom facilities, and cooking facilities. Dorm rooms are generally single sex. Many hostels have in-house tourist information services and they are a good place to network with budget travellers. Age is not a factor for staying in hostels.

Camping

Australia's campgrounds vary from fully serviced sites with all the amenities to dusty patches of earth with only a concrete toilet block. The average campground has tent sites, toilet and shower facilities, and water available. The better ones often have cabin-type accommodation and laundry facilities. Campgrounds in Australia generally do not have cooking facilities. Caravan Parks are campgrounds that include electric hook-ups and dumping facilities for caravans and motor homes (RV's).

Be aware of the dangers of flash floods, bush fires, and getting lost when camping out of designated camping areas. Permits are required for some areas and Fire Bans are often in effect. Rangers or the local police will be able to provide information on the hazards of specific areas.

Other Accommodation

Home and farm stays are an interesting alternative. Some include helping on the farm as part of your stay. Serviced apartments are available in major cities and resort towns and are popular with groups. Bed & Breakfasts are another option, but these are often quite expensive. Local tourist offices can provide information on these accommodations.

TRAVEL WITHIN AUSTRALIA

Plane

Qantas and Ansett are the two main domestic carriers. All major towns and tourist destinations are served by at least one of these airlines or their subsidiaries. The full price economy fare from Sydney to Perth is around $700, and the flight is about 5 hours. Bikes can normally be carried as personal luggage but check with the airline when booking. There is usually a surcharge for flying with a bike. Domestic airlines generally require bicycle tyres to be deflated, handle bars turned sideways, pedals removed or turned inwards, and the chain wrapped. Discounted fares (up to 50% off in some cases) are available by booking several weeks in advance, although once made sometimes these bookings cannot be changed. If you have flexibility in your travel arrangements standby seats are available on many routes at discounted rates (about 20% off).

Train

Services range from inner city to inter-state. All of Australia's major cities are linked by rail. The two famous long distance Australian routes are The Ghan, from Adelaide to Alice Springs (20 hours), and The Indian-Pacific which runs between Sydney and Perth (via Adelaide). The latter takes a whopping 64 hours, and includes the longest stretch of straight track in the world (478km). These long distance routes have sleepers (first class only), airline style recliner seats, and buffet cars. The one-way economy fare for the Indian-Pacific is $424 and there is a $30 fee for bicycles, which can be loaded directly into the baggage carriage. Austrail passes allow unlimited travel on trains within set limits and are available to foreign passport holders only. Contact Rail Australia for more information; Freephone 13 21 47 (in Australia) or (08) 8213 4592 (from overseas).

Bus

Bussing is cheaper than flying or rail travel, but in a country this big it takes a while to get anywhere. Bus services link all the major cities and many smaller towns across

Australia. The two big national service providers are Greyhound Pioneer and McCafferty's. Buses are air-conditioned and most have on-board toilets and reclining seats. Getting to Perth by bus involves a 24-hour trip from Sydney to Adelaide, then a 36.5-hour trip onto Perth (total about $340). Bikes will be carried but they need to be boxed and there is a surcharge. A good option for bus travel is one of the passes available for set-periods or set-distances, allowing considerable flexibility. For example, Greyhound offers a coast to coast pass for Sydney to Perth ($357), valid for 3 months, which lets you hop on and off as often as you like. There are also many bus operators offering package tours, some of them Outback adventure trips, which combine travel, accommodation, and meals.

Car

Avis, Budget and Hertz, are the three big car rental companies in Australia. There are also many smaller rental companies that offer competitive rates. Renting a car is an expensive way to travel around Australia. Rental plans usually offer unlimited kilometre plans in cities, and per kilometre packages for long distance and Outback travel. Some plans don't allow you to leave the state. If you want to carry a bike you'll need to hire a car big enough to fit your dismantled bike, or get a carry rack. Many companies have a minimum driver age of 25, or charge higher rates for drivers between 21 and 25. Insurance and damage waivers are generally included in the plan (as always, there are the occasional horror stories about huge charges for alleged damage to a rental). Petrol costs about 72c a litre. *See p.27 for details on driving in Australia.*

Other Transport

Hitch-hiking with a bike is a difficult way to get anywhere. Hitching in Australia is no more dangerous than elsewhere in the world, but it's still not recommended - a man called Ivan Millat was recently imprisoned for murdering tourists he picked up between Sydney and Canberra.

AUSTRALIAN TIME ZONES

Australia has 3 official time zones. Eastern Standard Time (EST) covers NSW, ACT, Qld., Vic., and Tas. and is 10 hours ahead of Greenwich Mean Time (GMT). Central Standard Time (CST) covers NT and SA and is 9.5 hours ahead of GMT (half an hour behind EST). Western Standard Time (WST) covers WA and is 8 hours ahead of GMT (2 hours behind EST and 1.5 hours behind CST). For example, when it's noon in Sydney, it's 11:30am in Adelaide, 10:00am in Perth. To make life easier for the locals living in eastern areas of WA there is also an unofficial 45-minute split in the time zone near Caiguna.

During summer most states move their clocks forward 1 hour and go to Daylight Saving Time (Qld. does not). Exactly when each state does this varies, but it's either in October or November, then in February or March they move out of Daylight Saving Time by putting their clocks back 1 hour.

BANKS, ATMS, AND EXCHANGE RATES

Banks are open weekdays from 9:30am to 4:00pm (5:00pm on Fridays). Most banks change foreign currency and cash traveller's cheques on the spot. ATMs are common in cities and large towns and provide cash advances on major credit cards and, depending on your ATM or debit card, access to your home bank account. Check the fees associated with using a particular ATM, and know the fees your own credit card company will charge if you intend getting cash advances.

At the time of this printing, the exchange rate for one Australian dollar was as follows:

Country	$A will purchase
UK	0.37
USA	0.54
Canada	0.83
New Zealand	1.29
Germany	1.20
France	4.02

Australia has 5c, 10c, 20c, and 50c silver coins, $1 and $2 gold coins, and $5, $10, $20, $50, and $100 notes. Major credit cards are widely accepted. Tipping is not required in Australia and most taxi drivers, doormen, and waiters do not expect to be tipped.

A new tax, the 10% Goods and Services Tax (GST), was added to most goods and services on 1 July, 2000.

SHOPPING

Normal trading hours are Monday to Friday 9:00am to 5:30pm, and Saturday 9:00am to 4:00pm. Late night shopping is usually on a Thursday or Friday till 9:00pm and some shops open Sundays. Restaurants, service stations, and corner stores have extended hours. The cheapest food prices are normally in supermarkets, rather than smaller stores and service stations (which often sell a limited range of food items). Some ballpark prices are as follows:

Loaf of bread	$2.60	Milk (1 litre)	$1.60
Bananas (1 kg)	$1.49	Cheese (500 g)	$4
Peanut butter (250 g)	$2.50	Mince (1 kg)	$7
Small chocolate bar	$1.40	Meat pie	$2.50
Big Mac	$2.75	Cup of coffee	$2
Sandwich	$3.50	Can of Coke	$1.50
35mm film 36 exp.	$12	Petrol (gas), 1litre regular	72c
Diesel (1 litre)	78c	Local phone call	40c
Internal letter rate	45c	30 min at Internet Cafe	$6
Movie ticket	$12	Compact disc	$30
Dorm bed at hostel	$18	Motel room (not in a city)	$50
Motel room (in a city)	$100	Bicycle inner tube	$10
Bicycle tire	$40		

COMMUNICATIONS

Telephones

A local call from a public phone box costs 40c for unlimited time. Most phone boxes accept coins or phone cards (which are widely available). Australia recently adopted an 8-digit phone number system across the country. 2-digit area codes are used in front of these 8-digit numbers. There are only four area codes: **02** for Sydney, Canberra, most of NSW, ACT, and some border areas of Vic. and Qld., **03** includes Melbourne and Hobart, and covers Tas., most of Vic., and some border areas of NSW, **07** covers Brisbane, Cairns, most of Qld., and some NSW border areas, and **08** covers Adelaide, Perth, Darwin, the whole of WA, NT, SA, and some border areas of NSW. Numbers starting with 800 or 1-800 are toll-free, and 13-prefixed numbers can be used to dial anywhere in Australia for the cost of a local call. International calls can be made from any phone with an International Direct Dial number or through the operator. For operator assistance dial 1223. For international toll-call costs dial 1255. Check on the costs for calls from hotels, operator-assisted calls, and the cheapest time of day to make long-distance and international calls. Using prepaid phone cards is generally the cheapest option.

When calling Australia from overseas; dial your international access code; 61 the country code for Australia; leave the 0 off the area code; then dial the 8-digit number.

Emergency calls to 000 are free.

Mail
Post offices are open Monday to Friday 9:00am to 5:00pm. The standard internal letter rate is 45c. Postcards to most countries cost $1. Letters up to 50g to New Zealand and SE Asia also cost $1. Letters up to 50g to North America, Europe, and the UK cost $1.50.

Post Offices have a Post Restante service that will receive and hold mail for one month, free of charge. This service can be a good way to rid yourself of excess weight as you cycle across the country (used maps, photographs, and tourist stuff can be posted ahead).

The Internet and E-mail
Public access to the Internet and e-mail can be difficult when travelling in Australia. Currently access is available at Internet cafes in major cities and in some of the larger towns. Public libraries, hotels, and hostels are slowly starting to offer these services.

TV, Radio, and The Press
The Australian Broadcasting Corporation (ABC) runs a Government funded, commercial-free, TV and radio (AM and FM) network that has the most widely available coverage across the country. Channels 7 and 9 are the other main free-to-air TV channels.

Each major city has its own newspaper. *The Sydney Morning Herald* and *The Melbourne Age* are the biggest selling non-tabloids and are found throughout the country. *The Bulletin* is a weekly news magazine, similar to *Time*, which has been published since 1880.

EMERGENCY CONTACTS

Dial 000 for Police, Ambulance, and Fire services. In an emergency (e.g. loss of passport, arrest, serious injury) your Embassy, High Commission, or Consulate in Australia can help with contacting relatives at home, and if you get into serious trouble, they may provide a temporary loan, which will have to be repaid. Your Embassy can also assist with repatriation in cases of emergency. Listings for some Embassies and Consular Offices are as follows. For others see the Yellow Pages under "Consulates and Legations".

1797 A strange creature, the platypus, is discovered in the Hawkesbury River

New Zealand

NZ High Commission, Commonwealth Ave, Yarralumla, Canberra, ACT, Ph (06) 270 4211

NZ Tourism Board, 644 Chapel St, Melbourne, Vic., Ph (03) 9823 6283

NZ Consulate General, 1 Alfred St, Circular Quay, Sydney, NSW, Ph (02) 9247 1999

There is also a NZ diplomatic office in Brisbane

US

US Embassy, Moonah Pl, Yarralumla, Canberra, ACT, Ph (02) 6214 5600

US Consulate General, 16 St George's Tce, Perth, WA, Ph (08) 9231 9400

US Consulate General, MLC Centre, Level 59, 19-29 Martin Pl, Sydney, NSW, Ph (02) 9373 9200

There is a US consulate in Melbourne

Canada

Canadian High Commission, Commonwealth Ave, Yarralumla, Canberra, ACT, Ph (02) 6270 4000

Canadian Consulate, 267 St George's Tce, Perth, WA, Ph (09) 322 7930

Canadian Consulate General, Level 5, Quay West Building, 111 Harrington St, Sydney, NSW, Ph (02) 364 3000

There is also a Canadian diplomatic office in Melbourne.

UK

British High Commission, Commonwealth Ave, Yarralumla, Canberra, ACT, Ph (02) 6270 6666

British Consulate, Level 16, The Gateway, 1 Macquarie Pl, Sydney, NSW, Ph (02) 9247 7521

British Consulate, Level 26, Allendale Sq, 77 St George's Tce, Perth, WA, Ph (08) 9221 4422

There are also UK diplomatic offices in Brisbane, Melbourne, Adelaide, and Hobart

France

Embassy of France, 6 Perth Ave, Yarralumla, Canberra, ACT, Ph (06) 6216 0100

There are also French diplomatic offices in Perth, Adelaide, Darwin, Brisbane, Melbourne, and Hobart

French Consulate General, 31 Market St, Sydney, NSW, Ph (02) 9261 5779

Germany

Embassy of FRG, 119 Empire Crt, Yarralumla, Canberra, ACT, Ph (02) 6270 1911

Japan

Embassy of Japan, 112 Empire Crt, Yarralumla, Canberra, ACT, Ph (02) 6273 3244

Japanese Consulate General, Level 21, The Forrest Centre, 221 St George's Tce, Perth, WA, Ph (09) 321 7816

Japanese Consulate General, Level 34, Colonial Centre, 52 Martin Pl., Sydney, NSW, Ph (09) 231 3455

There are also Japanese diplomatic offices in Brisbane and Melbourne.

1800 The European population at the turn of the century is 6,000

HOLIDAYS

Public Holidays

Banks, Government offices, schools and most businesses are closed on public holidays, which generally leads to an increase in road traffic. National public holidays are as follows (individual states also have their own public holidays):

Holiday	Date
New Years Day	January 1
Australia Day	January 26
Easter	Late March/Early April
	(Good Friday and Easter Monday)
ANZAC Day	April 25
Queen's Birthday	Second Monday in June
Labour Day	First Monday in October
Christmas Day	December 25
Boxing Day	December 26

School Holidays

The main school holiday break is traditionally mid-December through late-January (a 6-week summer break). There are also 2-week breaks in mid-April, late-June/early-July, and in late-September (the dates for these holidays vary between states). Domestic travel and accommodation in tourist areas can be difficult to book around these times.

WEIGHTS AND MEASURES

In 1972 Australia adopted the metric system. Temperatures are reported in Celsius, distances in metres and kilometres, weights in grams and kilograms, and volumes in litres and cubic metres. *See Appendix C for conversion between metric and imperial units.*

THE AUSSIE TOUNGE

Australia's rich vernacular is an insight into the country's social development, and away from the cities you hear some real gems. The following is a sampling of useful words and phrases:

Aussie, Auzzi, Oz; *Australia or Australian*
Beyond the black stump; *Very remote area*
Billabong; *An oxbow or waterhole*
Bludger; *A parasitic individual*
Bush; *Remote uninhabited area*
Cobber; *Good friend*
Digger; *Hard worker (also an Aussie soldier)*
Drongo; *A complete idiot*
Fair dinkum; *Absolutely true*
Galah; *An inept person (also a type of parrot)*
Hard yakka; *Hard work*
Outback; *Very remote inland area*
Sheila; *Woman*
Stubbies; *Bottled beer*
Tucker; *Food*
Whinger; *A complainer*

Back of beyond; *Very remote area*
Barbie; *BBQ*
Blowie; *Blow fly*
Bonza; *Excellent*
Chunder; *Vomit*
Damper; *Camp bread (unleavened)*
Dinkum; *True*
Dunny; *Toilet*
Fair dinkum?; *Really?*
G'day; *Hi (strangulation of "Good Day")*
Mozzie; *Mosquito*
Ocker; *A stereotypical Aussie male*
Smoko; *A work break*
Tinnies; *Canned beer*
Ute; *Utility vehicle (pick-up truck)*
Wop-wops; *Miles from anywhere*

1803 Matthew Flinders circumnavigates Australia, publishes "A Voyage to Terra Australis", and coins the name Australia

25

ON THE ROAD

Cycle Touring in Australia

Plan to carry enough water and food to be self-sufficient between the towns on this tour - plus a little in reserve. The longest unsupported stretch on this trip is the 192km between Norseman and Balladonia in WA and, like many of the remote areas along this route, there are no facilities between these settlements. Before you start, get an idea of your daily water consumption for touring, then, realising Australia is a hot country for cycling, be conservative. A minimum of 4 or 5 litres a day is not unreasonable. Service stations, hotels, motels, houses and farms will generally supply drinking water, but in many places water is a precious resource and you may have to pay for it (a sign behind the counter at the Balladonia roadhouse reads "Do Not Ask For Water As Refusal May Offend"). There are a few public water tanks placed along the Eyre Highway on the Nullarbor but these should not be relied on due to the possibility of vandalism. If you do use water from these tanks boil it first.

Be prepared to fix your bicycle yourself if it breaks down. There are few bike shops or spares to be found outside the main towns. Listings of bike shops along the route are included in Part II.

The busiest stretches of road on this tour are near the main cities: the Perth to Coolgardie leg, from Port Augusta to Adelaide, and from Bathurst to Sydney. Approaches to other large towns along the way also have a higher concentration of traffic. In rural areas cars and trucks travel fast. In particular road trains (articulated trucks towing two or three trailers) passing at speed can create a strong wind that requires you to have a firm grip of the handlebars to resist. There are the usual hazards for cyclists in cities - watch for car doors opening and drivers not anticipating bicycles. Most Australian drivers are courteous towards cyclists. A tiny fraction, for whatever reason, are not - these are the ones who yell, honk, or drive dangerously near cyclists. The best policy is to ignore these people, or report them to the Police if they behave dangerously.

In 1990 Australia became the first country to introduce a mandatory helmet law for cyclists (New Zealand followed soon after). Basically the law requires a helmet to be worn while riding on the road and you can be fined for failure to do so. There was some debate over the introduction of this law but helmets are now widely used and it's unlikely the law will be repealed.

For night riding a white headlight and red taillight are legal requirements. Touring in the dark is not recommended.

In this guide the topography along the route is discussed in general terms in the text, and is summarised on the stage profiles. Not every climb is mentioned. In the text the terrain is described (in increasing steepness) as flat, gently rolling, rolling, or hilly. Flat terrain may include a few climbs and descents but when these are present they are generally gentle. Terrain described as gently rolling includes gentle rises and falls with occasional moderate climbs but rarely any steep climbs. Rolling countryside includes moderate and some steep climbs, and hilly terrain is just that; hilly and hard going. Of course wind direction, weather conditions, and an individual's fitness are strong influences, and a tough head wind can make even flat terrain hard going.

The 100km photographs in this guide will give you an idea of the type of country that you will travel through on the tour (Note: The accumulated distance for these photographs includes the minor detours required to ride to and from accommodation and nearby shops).

*1806 Captain Bligh is appointed 4th Governor of NSW on
the recommendation of Sir Joseph Banks*

ROADS AND MAPS

The Australian roading system consists of freeways, highways, and major and minor roads. Freeways are in, or near, the major cities, and bicycles are generally prohibited. Signs at the on-ramps and off-ramps indicate where bikes must exit as a freeway approaches the city.

A network of highways links the main towns across Australia. These have names like the Great Eastern Highway or the Mid-Western Highway, or are named after respected pioneers like the Eyre Highway or Sturt Highway. These routes are sealed (mostly a bitumen and chip surface), are generally single laned, and the lanes are not divided. Crossroads typically intersect directly with the highway. Highways are the quickest route between rural towns but can be busy. For cyclists, the edges of highways can vary from a wide smooth shoulder to the left of a painted strip, to little or no shoulder at all, however there is normally enough room to ride comfortably in traffic.

Major roads are similar to highways but link smaller towns, and minor roads can be sealed or unsealed and sometimes dead-end in the Outback.

Each state has the responsibility for maintaining their own roads, and as their maintenance cycles vary, you'll notice the condition of the road changes between states. In general Australia's roads are well maintained, although heat and heavy traffic sometimes cause bulging and breaking at the edges where cyclists spend most of their time.

In terms of maps, most of this route is on highways which are easy to follow and well signposted (in rural areas there are often no other sealed roads to follow!), however, the Australian Automobile Association does provide good touring maps and AUSLIG (Australia's national mapping agency) provides topographic maps at various scales e.g. 1:250,000 (540 maps cover the whole country), 1:100,000, and partial coverage at 1:50,000. AUSLIG's maps are available directly (AUSLIG Map Shop, Scrivener Building, Dunlop Court, Fern Hill Park, Bruce, ACT 2617, Ph (02) 6201 4201, Fax: (02) 6201 4366), or from map retailers throughout the country.

AUSSIE TRAFFIC - SOME ROAD RULES

Australians drive on the **left** so remember to **look right first** when coming to intersections or stepping out onto the road. Each state has its own road rules (e.g. there is no speed limit in parts of NT), but some rules apply almost everywhere, for example at intersections **give way to the right** means every vehicle on your right has priority. In addition, when you are **turning right** you must **give way to oncoming traffic turning left**. At **Stop** and **Give Way** signs you give way to everyone. All speed and distance signs are in kilometres.

Most roundabouts and traffic islands have signs. When there are no signs, the "give way to the right" rule applies (you also have to give way to all traffic already in a round about).

Traffic accidents involving injury must be reported to the Police as soon as possible, and within 24 hours. If questioned by the Police, the law requires you to give your name, address, and proof of identification. You are not obliged to make a statement at the accident scene. Australia strictly enforces its drink-driving laws, and seatbelts are compulsory for drivers and passengers.

The Police and the Australian Automobile Association can supply information on the road rules. Within the Automobile Association each state has its own Automobile Club which produces publications and provides advice on traffic and travel issues.

HAZARDS

Australia's desert and semi-arid regions are big and harsh. Running out of water, food, or shade can be fatal. Don't venture off-road or into Outback areas unaccompanied, ill equipped, or without talking to the local authorities. Be aware of the potential for bush fires in the areas you are travelling. The fire hazard is usually broadcast in the media, and Fire-Bans are sometimes enforced. Flash flooding can occur in low-lying Outback areas so don't camp in dry riverbeds, and Willy-Willys (brief dust storms) occasionally occur in deserts and neighbouring areas.

Australia's snakes are legendary and justifiably feared, but they are generally shy and only strike if threatened. Don't walk barefoot in long grass or poke around wood stacks or places snakes might lurk. Two venomous spiders that are dangerous to humans are the Red-Back, and around Sydney, the Funnel-Web. Australia's list of biters and stingers also includes scorpions, centipedes, ants, ticks, wasps, mosquitoes, sand flies, and bees. Waterborne hazards include the East Coast's Box-jellyfish, and in northern Australia both freshwater and saltwater crocodiles.

One annoying species for cyclists is the Magpie. When nesting (between June and December depending on the region) these black and white crows vigorously defend their roadside territory by swooping on passers-by. The distraction can be enough to cause a cyclist to take a tumble or swerve into traffic. The birds, however, rarely make contact and always retreat once you've passed through their road space.

Other road users are probably the biggest hazard to cycle tourists - ride with safety in mind and, as in any country, be conscious of your personal security around others.

There is also a psychological aspect to cycle touring in a country as big and unpopulated as Australia - for some the remote and undeveloped areas are the biggest attraction, but for others the thought of crossing these isolated expanses by pedal power can be overwhelming.

BICYCLE CLUBS AND ORGANIZATIONS

Bicycle Clubs
Several bicycle clubs have a focus on touring and offer club-run events. These clubs are also a good source of local information. Several are listed below. In addition, most major towns and many smaller towns have local bicycle clubs focused on road racing and/or mountain biking. Make enquiries at the local library or tourist information centre.

CTA - The Cycle Touring Association of WA: Take recreational day rides and run tours. Contact: On Your Bike WA, PO Box 282, Inglewood, WA 6052

Cycling 4 Pleasure: A club of recreational and touring cyclists which organises day, weekend, and week long tours in WA. Contact: Cycling 4 Pleasure, PO Box 883, Victoria Park, WA 6879

Audax Australia: Runs timed tours over short and long distances both on- and off-road. Contact: See the Internet at: *www.audax.org.au*

Bicycle Advocacy
The Bicycle Federation of Australia (BFA) is a national body that focuses on the interests of cyclists and conducts campaigns to promote cycling. The BFA, among other things,

1813 Gregory Blaxland succeeds in crossing the Blue Mountains

lobbies for bike lanes and cycle paths. They can be contacted at:

The Bicycle Federation of Australia, GPO Box 3222, Canberra, ACT 2601, Ph (02) 6355 1570, Fax (02) 6355 7524

BIKE TOUR OPERATORS

A number of companies offer package bicycle touring holidays in Australia. These range from Outback adventure trips to luxury excursions through relaxing rural areas. If you are inexperienced in cycle touring, organised tours are a good option as you are part of a group and much of the planning is done for you. The drawbacks are that they are more expensive than touring independently and generally require you to travel at the pace of the group. Operators include:

Remote Outback Cycle Tours: Offer fully supported bike tours with a mix of cycling and 4-wheel driving. Their trips range from 4 to 10 days, and options include the Alice Springs area, Kakadu, the Oodnadatta Track, and portions of the Nullarbor. Contact: ROC Tours Australia Ltd, PO Box 1179, West Leederville, WA 6901, Ph (08) 9244 4614

Rolling On: Runs mountain bike tours in SA. Their tours all start from Adelaide and range from short trips to 15 days. Food is provided and accommodation is in cabins or camping. Contact: Rolling On, PO Box 19, Hove, SA 5048

Australian Bicycle Getaways: Specialise in luxury tours with 4-star accommodation and gourmet meals. They run tours in rural and coastal NSW ranging from 10 to 19 days. Contact: Australian Bicycle Getaways, PO Box 36, Beresfield, NSW 2322, Ph (02) 4964 1256, Fax (02) 4966 1579.

The East Coast Touring Cycling Club: A non-commercial club run by the same people that offer the more expensive Australian Bicycle Getaway trips (see above). These tours are low cost, catered, and involve camping. They run road and mountain biking trips on the East Coast centred around a base camp with a range of day rides offered. They also offer conventional tours up to 9 days long. Contact: See Australian Bicycle Getaways above.

GETTING TO/FROM PERTH AND SYDNEY AIRPORTS

There are scheduled bus, shuttle bus, and taxi services between the airports and downtown areas in Perth and Sydney. In Sydney there is also a train service ($9). One way to travel from the airport to the city centre with a bike is by shuttle bus. For around $15 a shuttle will take you and your bike from the airport to the door of your accommodation (although this often includes stops at other passenger's accommodation along the way). If you want to ride your bike directions are as follows:

Perth
The domestic and international terminals at Perth Airport are quite separate. It is about 15km from the international terminal, and about 10km from the domestic terminal, to downtown Perth.

From the domestic terminal take Brearley Ave to the Great Eastern Highway. Go left on the Great Eastern Highway, then right onto the causeway over the Swan River and straight-ahead onto Adelaide Tce, which leads into downtown Perth.

1816 Sydney's "Rum Hospital" opens. The contractor building the hospital in return for the exclusive rights to import rum

29

From the international terminal take Horrie Miller Rd, which crosses Tonkin Hwy and becomes Kewdale Rd. Continue on Kewdale Rd, then take a right onto Welshpool Rd. Continue straight-ahead on Welshpool Rd, which becomes the Albany Highway and crosses the Swan River. After crossing the river continue straight on Adelaide Tce into downtown.

Sydney

The downtown area is about 9km north of Sydney Airport. Exit the international terminal via Airport Dr and follow it until it joins the road from the domestic terminal at O'Riordan St. Head north on O'Riordan St, crossing Botany Rd, then turn left onto Elizabeth St. Continue on Elizabeth St which eventually becomes Phillip St by the Endeavour Fountain in downtown Sydney. Phillip St ends at Circular Quay on the shores of Sydney Harbour.

LAYOUT OF THIS GUIDE

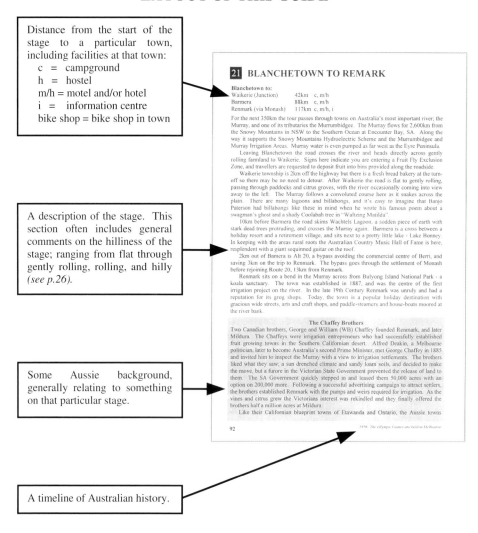

Distance from the start of the stage to a particular town, including facilities at that town:
c = campground
h = hostel
m/h = motel and/or hotel
i = information centre
bike shop = bike shop in town

A description of the stage. This section often includes general comments on the hilliness of the stage; ranging from flat through gently rolling, rolling, and hilly (see p.26).

Some Aussie background, generally relating to something on that particular stage.

A timeline of Australian history.

30

were designed to be free from the sale of intoxicating liquor. In rural Australia this caused a few ruffles and the SA Government rapidly legislated a change. The settlements started promisingly but the financial crisis of 1893 caused the demand for citrus to drop and as settlers left rabbits moved in. The brother's irrigation trust went broke and they lost everything. George went back to California (borrowing the return fare) but WB stayed on, working as a hired labourer. He managed to keep 90 acres, which he faithfully tended, and convinced other growers to join him in a co-operative. He also gave up teetotalling and started a distillery. Things eventually recovered and the irrigation towns went on to great prosperity. WB's dried fruit co-op and distillery blossomed, eventually becoming the biggest in Australia, and he was elected Mildura's first mayor. Back in the U.S., George regrew his fortune too, built on water rights and banking. WB was buried in Mildura, while George was laid to rest near San Diego overlooking the Pacific.

Camping:
Waikerie Caravan Park, Peake Tce. Waikerie, Ph (08) 8541 2651, T$11 ◻ Lake Bonney Caravan Park, Lakeside Drv, Barmera, Ph (08) 8588 2234, T$11 ◻ Renmark Riverfront Caravan Park, Sturt Hwy, Renmark, Ph (08) 8586 6315, T$12 ◻ Riverbend Park, Sturt Hwy Renmark, Ph (08) 8595 5131, T$12 ◻ Others: Waikerie, Barmera, Berri, Renmark

Motel/Hotel:
Waikerie Hotel-Motel, 2 McCoy St, Waikerie, Ph (08) 8541 2999, S$40, D$50 ◻ Barmera Hotel Motel, Barwell Ave, Barmera, Ph (08) 8588 2111, S$30,

D$40 ◻ Renmark Hotel-Motel, Murray Ave, Renmark, Ph (08) 8586 6755, S$50, D$60 ◻ Fountain Gardens Motel, Renmark Ave, Renmark, Ph (08) 8586 6899, S$50, D$60 ◻ Others: Waikerie, Barmera, Berri, Renmark (also a Hostel at Berri)

i:
Renmark/Paringa Visitor Centre, Murray Ave, Renmark, Ph (08) 8586 6704 ◻ Others: Berri

Bike Shop:
Nearest: Riverland Cycles, 22 Wilson St, Berri, Ph (08) 8582 1675

3000km 19km before Barmera

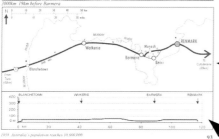

1959 Australia's population reaches 10,000,000

93

PART II
THE JOURNEY

PERTH

The crystal-clear air and faint eucalypt scent seem to cleanse this already modern city and make it sparkle. Built largely on the back of mineral wealth won from the unforgiving interior, Perth is a pleasant blend of old and new buildings.

The city's **civic centre** and main **shopping area** are bounded by Wellington, King, and Pier St's and St George's Tce. A trip down St George's Tce provides a good perspective on Perth's development. Starting at the western end there is WA's **Parliament House** (tours by appointment), **The Cloisters** (the façade from Perth's first Boys' High School now fronting a retail centre), and the colonial **National Trust** building. A 1980's addition is the **Bankwest Tower**, Perth's tallest building, which incorporates the Victorian **Palace Hotel** (now offices) with its fine ironwork balconies. Continuing east there is **St George Cathedral** (1850's) and next door; **Government House** built in Gothic style in the 1860's. **His Majesty's Theatre** is also worth a look.

Just to the north of downtown is the **Perth Cultural Centre**, which includes the **WA Museum**, the **Art Gallery of WA**, and the city's **Alexander Library**. Sports fans should try to catch a game of Australian Rules Football or cricket at the **WACA**.

Two blocks south of the city centre is the wide blue **Swan River**. Boats depart from the **Barrack St Jetty** for cruises to **wineries** up-river, and out to **Rottnest Is.** - a popular tourist trip. The river was an attraction for Aboriginal tribes long before Europeans arrived, and artefacts estimated to be 38,000 years old have been found on the riverbanks.

The Dutch were the first Europeans to sight WA. In 1616 Dirk Hartog was sailing a supply ship to Batavia (now Jakarta) when he was blown off course and sighted an unreported coastline. He sailed briefly down Australia's West Coast near Shark Bay, landed on an offshore island, and left a pewter plate to mark his visit. Dutch seamen

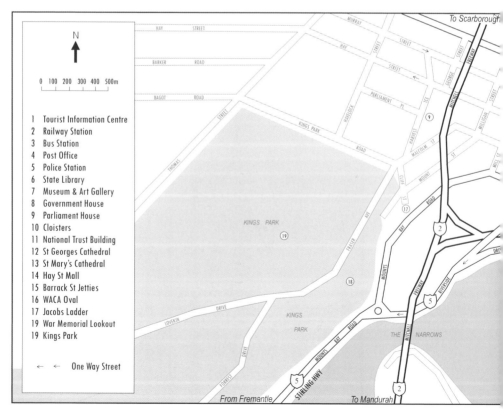

1 Tourist Information Centre
2 Railway Station
3 Bus Station
4 Post Office
5 Police Station
6 State Library
7 Museum & Art Gallery
8 Government House
9 Parliament House
10 Cloisters
11 National Trust Building
12 St Georges Cathedral
13 St Mary's Cathedral
14 Hay St Mall
15 Barrack St Jetties
16 WACA Oval
17 Jacobs Ladder
19 War Memorial Lookout
19 Kings Park

← ← One Way Street

1829 Perth is founded

continued to map this coastline with an eye to colonial expansion until the British ship *Tyral* also blundered into WA in 1622 and the secret of a new southern land was out.

In 1697 the Dutch captain Willem de Vlamingh explored the area around Perth, naming the river after the black swans he saw (white being the only colour known till then). He left, taking several swans with him (which died in transit), and headed back to Java, stopping on the way to pick up Hartog's plate and leaving behind another detailing both expeditions (the first plate is in Amsterdam, the second is in the WA museum).

Perth's best attraction is **Kings Park**, 400-hectares of virgin parkland overlooking downtown. Every spring the park's wildflowers put on a spectacular free show.

Camping:
Perth Holiday Park, 91 Benara Rd, Caversham, Ph (08) 9279 6700, T$11 (15km NE of downtown Perth) ⬜ Karrinyup Waters Resort, 467 North Beach Rd, Gwelup, Ph 1800 633 665, T$16, (13km N of downtown Perth) ⬜ Perth International Tourist Park, Hale Rd, Forrestfield, Ph (08) 9453 6677, T$20 (15km SE of downtown Perth) ⬜ Others; Perth

Hostel:
Britannia International YHA, 253 William St, Perth, Ph (08) 9328 6121, Dm$16, S$22, D$50 ⬜ Ozi Inn, 282 Newcastle St, Perth, Ph (08) 9328 1222, Dm$16, S$40, D$40 ⬜ Fremantle YHA, 11 Pakenham St, Fremantle, Ph (08) 9431 7065, Dm$14, S$20, D$34 ⬜ Cheviot Marina Backpackers, 4 Beach St, Fremantle, Ph (08) 9433 2055, Dm$15, D$39 ⬜ Others; Perth, Fremantle

Motel/Hotel:
Perth City Hotel, 200 Hay St, Perth, Ph (08) 9220 7000, S$83, D$83 ⬜ Baileys Parkside Motel, 150 Bennett St, Perth, Ph (08) 9325 3788, S$60, D$76 ⬜ Norfolk Hotel, 47 South Tce, Fremantle, Ph (08) 9335 5405, S$40, D$60 ⬜ Pier 21 Resort, 7 John St, Fremantle, Ph (08) 9336 2555, S$110, D$140 ⬜ Others; Perth, Fremantle

i:
WA Tourist Centre, Cnr Forrest Pl. & Wellington St (Next to PO), Perth, Ph 1300 361 351 ⬜ Fremantle Tourist Information Centre, Marine Tce, Fremantle, Ph (08) 9431 7878

Bike Shops:
Cycle Centre, 282 Hay St, Perth, Ph (08) 9325 1176 ⬜ Fleet Cycles, 66 Adelaide St, Fremantle, Ph (08) 9430 5414 ⬜ Others; Perth, Fremantle

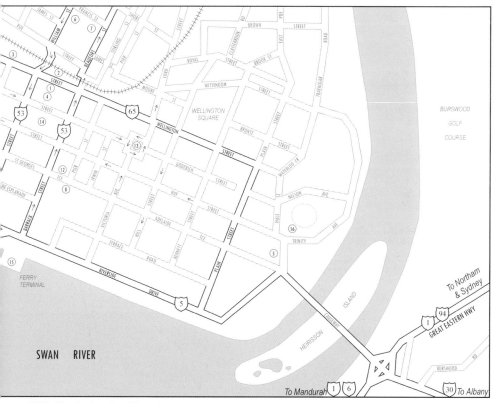

SWAN RIVER

1830's The Aboriginal and Non-Aboriginal populations are estimated to be equal.

1 FREMANTLE TO NORTHAM

Fremantle to:

Perth	19km	c, h, m/h, i, bike shop

Perth to:

Mundaring	35km	h, m/h, i, bike shop
Bakers Hill	67km	c
Clackline	81km	
Northam	99km	c, h, m/h, i, bike shop

This stage starts in Fremantle, or "Freo" as the locals call it, and passes through Kings Park and downtown Perth before crossing the Darling Ranges to Northam - a total of 118km.

You can ride to Fremantle or take a commuter train from Perth. Bicycles can be wheeled directly onto the trains, where surfers with boards ride next to businessmen with briefcases. Exit the Fremantle Railway Station and go right down Phillimore St, left onto Mouat St, then right onto Marine Parade, which leads down to Bathers Beach.

Bathers Beach is a small scallop of sand on the Indian Ocean, worth dipping your feet in before starting eastward towards the Pacific Ocean. Next to Bathers Beach is the Royal Perth Yacht Club, the site of the 1987 America's Cup defence. To start the tour head back up Marine Parade, left onto Pakenham St, and right onto High St through downtown Fremantle. You may have to walk your bike a couple of blocks here, as parts of the main street are one-way only. Continue straight on High St, which becomes Adelaide St then Quarry St. Turn left at the end of Quarry St onto Burt St, then right at the traffic lights onto the Stirling Highway which leads back to Perth. A longer but quieter route to Perth is via the city's network of cycle paths (tourist centres have maps).

Near downtown, opposite the University of WA, the entrance to Kings Park is signposted. The park is full of fragrant eucalypts and native birds darting above the road, and has sweeping views over Perth. Exit the park via Mount or Malcolm St's; both join St George's Tce, which passes through the CBD. Continue straight on St George's Tce, which becomes Adelaide Tce, crosses the Swan River and joins the Great Eastern Highway, a busy thoroughfare leaving the city. At Midland a solid 10km climb starts at the foot of the Darling Ranges. The road crosses a buried fault here, where the Archean granites of the Ranges have been uplifted above the younger sedimentary rocks of the Perth Plain.

By Mundaring the houses have thinned out, leaving scrappy brush dotted with distinctive Black-Boy trees. Gradually the climb levels out into rolling countryside with paddocks cut into the bush, although the road still has enough short steep hills to sap most of your energy before a gentle downhill into Northam. The town is on the Avon River and is a popular destination for kayakers. It also has WA's only white swans.

Gold and Water

A silver pipeline runs beside the road from Mundaring to Kalgoorlie. Charles O'Connor was the visionary behind this pipeline - The Coolgardie Water Supply Scheme. By 1894 gold discoveries had created inland boomtowns at Coolgardie and Kalgoorlie and the area was fabulously rich, unfortunately it was also bone dry. Entrepreneurial water traders had found a supply of shallow brackish water and built condensers to purify the precious liquid before selling it to the thirsty miners and their families at exorbitant prices. At one stage the water traders intentionally restricted the water supply until the miners were nearly out then, shrewdly they thought, doubled the price. The result was an ugly riot down Bayley Street, Coolgardie - culminating in a bonfire crowned with an effigy of a water trader. After the riot the Government stepped in and built its own

1830 Policy towards the Australian colonies shifts towards encouraging free settlers

condenser, the biggest ever built, but a reliable source of water was still a major problem.

As Engineer of Public Works Charles O'Connor had already designed Fremantle Harbour and rebuilt the rail line through the Darling Ranges, but his plan for a 600km water pipeline, including 8 steam powered pumping stations, to lift water 355m up to Calgoorlie was ridiculed by politicians and The Press. O'Conner fought for funding and in 1898 work eventually began. Water flowed along the pipeline for the first time in 1903 and the scheme was a huge success. The upgraded pipeline is still in use today. O'Connor never saw his vision completed though, worn down by the constant criticism he took his own life on Fremantle Beach 10 months before the pipeline was finished.

(Note: For Fremantle and Perth details see p.35)

Camping:
Bakers Hill Caravan Park, Great Eastern Hwy, <u>Bakers Hill</u>, Ph (08) 9574 1530, T$5 ☐ Mortlock Caravan Park, Great Eastern Hwy, <u>Northam</u>, Ph (08) 9622 1620, T$6 ☐ Others; <u>Midland</u>

Hostel:
Perth Hills YHA, Mundaring Weir Road, <u>Mundaring</u>, Ph (08) 9295 1809, Dm$14 ☐ Northam Guest House, 51 Wellington St, <u>Northam</u>, Ph (08) 9622 2301, S$20 ☐ Prospect Guest House, 402 Fitzgerald St, <u>Northam</u>, Ph (08) 9622 3152 *(re-opening mid-2001)*

Motel/Hotel:
Mundaring Weir Hotel, Mundaring Weir Rd, <u>Mundaring</u>, Ph (08) 9295 1106, D$82-$170 ☐

Commercial Hotel Motel, 190 Fitzgerald St, <u>Northam</u>, Ph (08) 9622 1049, S$20-$45, D$50 ☐ Northam Motel, 13 John St, <u>Northam</u>, Ph (08) 9622 1755, S$50 ☐ Others; <u>Mundaring</u>, <u>Northam</u>

i:
Mundaring Tourism Association, Great Eastern Hwy <u>Mundaring</u>, Ph (08) 9295 0202 ☐ Northam Tourist Information Bureau, 2 Grey St, <u>Northam</u>, Ph (08) 9622 2100

Bike Shops:
Mundaring Cycles, 7095 Great Eastern Hwy, <u>Mundaring</u>, Ph (08) 9295 2042 ☐ The Bike Shop, 82 Fitzgerald St, <u>Northam</u>, Ph (08) 9622 3434 ☐ Others; <u>Midland</u>

0km Bathers Beach, Fremantle

100km Between Clackline and Northam

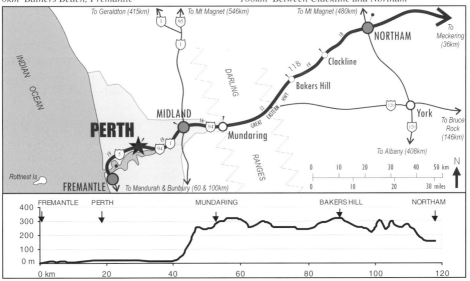

2 NORTHAM TO KELLERBERRIN

Northam to:

Meckering	36km	i
Cunderdin	59km	c, m/h
Tammin	83km	m/h
Kellerberrin	106km	c, m/h, i

Leaving Northam on the Great Eastern Highway the road enters WA's wheat belt - a sometimes-productive strip of land between the coast and the desert. In springtime the roadside fields are usually full of symmetrical lines of swaying green shoots, but during droughts the crops are liable to completely fail, and sheep are let loose in the paddocks.

The road is flat to gently rolling and crosses vast fields with little sign of human habitation. The occasional houses are far from the road in tiny islands of trees surrounded by paddocks. Meckering consists of a scattering of squat buildings with a lot of open space between them. A sign in a field just outside town hints at why there aren't any substantial buildings - a massive earthquake in 1968 levelled the town. The sign sits on the fault line although it's pretty hard to envisage a flatter, more stable looking, piece of earth. Cunderdin has a service station and a few agricultural type shops with improbable looking machinery on display. Further down the road at Tammin it's possible to ride through the town at midday, past the railway station, the grain silos, and several service stations, and not see a soul.

The road gently drops the last 10km into Kellerberin, another agricultural service town. The main street is lined down one side by old wooden buildings, and on the other side by the Perth-Kalgoorlie rail line. Over the rail line, on the outskirts of town, past tin roofed houses with shady verandas and barking dogs, is the town campground. Tucked into a corner of the showgrounds, this is bare bones Australian camping - a concrete toilet and shower block and a patch of red earth, the cost: $2 per person. The caretaker, who has an impressive set of tattoos on his arms, hands, and fingers, can tell you about some of the cyclists he has seen pass through - the Japanese guy who rode in from the Nullarbor in mid-summer, when the hottest winds blow, apparently on some kind of company endurance test, and the American couple who both had nervous breakdowns here after riding up from Perth. Rising out of the flat next to the showgrounds is an interesting rock outcrop, worth the climb if you have any energy left.

The Kangaroo

Long before you see a live kangaroo in Australia you are, unfortunately, liable to see and smell a dead one on the roadside. Kangaroos are plentiful, have no regard for roads, and are most active at dawn and dusk, so invariably some of these curious, graceful, creatures get hit by traffic. Colliding with a 120kg kangaroo at speed is no trifling thing, and most rural folk and all the truckers have precautionary "Roo bars" on their vehicles.

Kangaroos belong to the Marsupial order, which completely dominates Australia's native mammal population thanks to a split from Gondwana before other mammals arrived. Australia's isolation meant that marsupials, which give birth prematurely and raise their young in a pouch, avoided having to compete with the later arrival of placental mammals (which support their young via a placenta). So while antelope and deer graze the plains of other continents, kangaroos and their relations fill this niche in Australia.

The kangaroo has an ingenious reproductive system for the variable climate of the Australian bush. Born after about 33 days the tiny, blind, and still developing "joey" crawls along a path licked in her fur by the mother, and into the pouch where it attaches itself to a teat for several months before resurfacing. After giving birth female kangaroos

1836 William Light chooses the site for Adelaide

can immediately mate again. This means a female may be pregnant, as well as having a tiny pink newborn and a ridiculously large older joey in her pouch all at the same time. Interestingly, the mother's milk supplied to each teat is different depending on the joey's development. All this reproductive technology uses a lot of energy, so during tough periods of drought when food is scarce the female kangaroo is also able to switch off her reproductive cycle, effectively "freezing" an embryo. When it rains or food becomes available the system is switched back on and development of the embryo recommences.

Aside from its curious scientific attributes the kangaroo is just plain beautiful with its soft fur, liquid eyes, and distinctive gait. Sadly, on Outback farms where grass is a valuable resource, the kangaroo's ability to graze the land and breed so successfully make it a serious pest and, if licensed, farmers are within their rights to shoot them. This national icon is also professionally hunted for its pelt, for pet food, and for the menu of posh restaurants across Australia.

Camping:
Cunderdin Caravan Park, 74 Olympic Ave, Cunderdin, Ph (08) 9635 1258, T$10 ☐ Kellerberrin Caravan Park, Kellerberrin Showgrounds, Kellerberrin, Ph (08) 9045 4066, T$2

Motel/Hotel:
Cunderdin Motor-Hotel, Main St, Cunderdin, Ph (08) 9635 1104, S$45, D$65 ☐ Tammin Hotel, Donnan St, Tammin, Ph (08) 9637 1004, S$35, D$45 ☐ Kellerberrin Hotel Motel, 108 Massingham St,

Kellerberrin, Ph (08) 9045 4206, S$30, D$40 ☐ Shell Roadhouse Motel, 150 Massingham St, Kellerberrin, Ph (08) 9045 4007, S$40, D$50 ☐ Others; Kellerberrin

i:
The Big Camera Photography Museum, 11 Dreyer St, Meckering, Ph (08) 9625 1335 ☐ Kellerberrin Tourist Centre, 110 Massingham St, Kellerberrin, Ph (08) 9045 4006

200km Between Cunderdin and Tammin

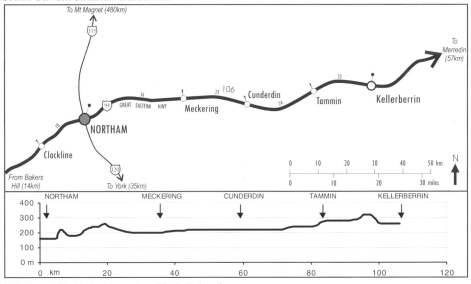

3 KELLERBERRIN TO CARRABIN

Kellerberrin to:

Merredin	57km	c, m/h, i
Burracoppin	81km	
Carrabin	100km	c, m/h

The Great Eastern Highway is flat to gently rolling between Kellerberrin and Carrabin. The road is a single lane in each direction, the painted edges sloughing off under the barrage of truck tyres. The seal is fringed by wide dirt strips pocked with thousands of ant holes. Each tiny ant volcano continuously erupts as ants climb out, drop a grain of sand over the edge, turn around and disappear back inside. The countryside is farmed, but you get the impression it is becoming progressively more difficult to tame the land as you head inland. Beside the road is the water pipeline and a string of power poles - lifelines to Coolgardie and Kalgoorlie.

Merredin started out as a stopping point for miners on their way to the goldfields. Now it's a town of about 3,000 serving the surrounding agricultural areas. In a water saving coup this town was the first in Australia to treat sewage wastewater and use it for watering their recreational grounds. The town has a rail museum detailing the development of the area. Past Merriden the network of roads off the main highway rapidly drops away and Kalgoorlie becomes the principal destination.

Burracoppin, with a solitary pub and phone box, is more of a location than a settlement, but it is significant in that WA's first vermin proof fence crosses the highway here. These fences were an early attempt to hold back the westward spread of rabbits and were installed following a 1901 Perth Royal Commission into rabbit control.

A welcome sign appears 2km before Carrabin indicating a caravan park, meals, and fuel. Unfortunately, at Carrabin, which consists of a solitary service station, another sign points to the caravan park 8km to the north. The service station does however have a basic roadhouse with a diner, box-like cabins and a dusty camping area. A constant stream of cars runs down the highway and the forecourt bell is continually ringing as vehicles stop for fuel. Despite the limited facilities the sunsets are beautiful.

The Longest Fences in the World

When the clipper *Lightning,* sailing from England, docked at Melbourne in 1859 there was a consignment of 12 wild rabbits aboard for a certain Thomas Austin. A successful Melbourne businessman, Austin had decided he needed some sport at Barwon Park, his estate on the outskirts of town. He was either a bad shot, or the rabbits multiplied faster than he could shoot them, because seven years later they were observed as far away as Qld., and by 1895 they were at Eucla in WA. Pastoralists quickly noticed the rabbits' impact - as the grass cover reduced so did the number of stock the land could support. In some areas vegetation patterns changed completely and erosion became a big problem.

With a gestation period of just 30 days, the rabbits were able to have over 10 successive litters a year during favourable conditions, and the Government faced a serious dilemma. State Rabbit Boards were formed and fences thousands of kilometres long were erected to stop the spreading infestation. WA's No. 1 Rabbit-Proof Fence, running the length of the state, was completed in 1907, and the No. 2 fence near Cunderdin soon followed as a second line of defence. The fences failed to stop the westward advance. Sometimes they were erected after rabbits had crossed, they were difficult to maintain, and there were rumours that some fences were deliberately broken by those with a vested interest in seeing the rabbits spread. Even with the fences in place there were stories of crazed hordes of rabbits piling up against the fence to the extent that

1847 An overland mail service commences between Melbourne and Adelaide

others could climb over.

A break-through in rabbit control came in the summer of 1950 when the government allowed the introduction of the South American mosquito borne virus Myxomatosis. The disease spread rapidly with a rabbit mortality of 99.9% in places, and the nation's wool and meat production jumped as a result. But the rabbits fought back by developing genetic resistance and the virus itself weakened into less virulent strains. By the early 1990's scientists and the farmers were pinning their hopes on a new biological control - rabbit calicivirus - which was being tested in a quarantine facility offshore from Adelaide. Somehow the disease escaped to the mainland where it quickly infected and killed an estimated 200 million rabbits. It proved to be so effective that the virus was smuggled across the Tasman to New Zealand farms in spite of bio-security regulations.

Thomas Austin's legacy is an ecological disaster that continues to be a problem for Australia's farmers. The fences are still maintained in places, although now mainly to reduce the spread of dingoes and kangaroos into farmed areas.

Camping:
Merredin Caravan Park, Oats St (Cnr Great Eastern Hwy) <u>Merredin</u>, Ph (08) 9041 1535, T$11 ▯ Carrabin Roadhouse, Great Eastern Highway, <u>Carrabin</u>, Ph (08) 9046 7162, T$ = a few dollars for use of showers

Eastern Hwy, <u>Merredin</u>, Ph (08) 9041 1755, S$55, D$65 ▯ Carrabin Roadhouse, Great Eastern Highway, <u>Carrabin</u>, Ph (08) 9046 7162, S$39, D$49 ▯ Others; <u>Merredin</u>

Motel/Hotel:
Merredin Motel, 10 Gamenya Ave, <u>Merredin</u>, Ph (08) 9041 1886, S$45, D$50 ▯ Potts Motor Inn, Great

i:
Merredin Tourist Centre, Barrack Street, <u>Merredin</u>, Ph (08) 9041 1666

300km 1km past Merridin

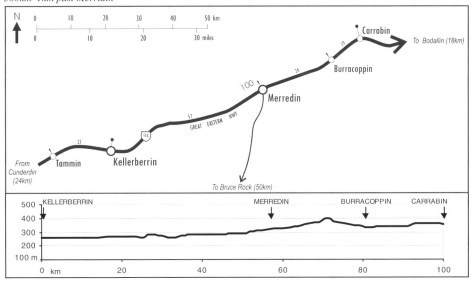

1848 Ludwig Leichhardt, a German naturalist, leads an expedition to cross central Australia E to W. His party departs and is never heard from or seen again

41

4 CARRABIN TO YELLOWDINE

Carrabin to:

Bodallin	18km
Moorine Rock	45km m/h
Southern Cross	66km c, m/h, i
Yellowdine	100km c, m/h

Continuing eastward from Carrabin the road gently climbs for about 10km before Bodallin, a tiny settlement with no facilities. The road varies between flat and gently rolling the rest of the way to Yellowdine.

Moorine Rock is 45km from Carrabin, although the rock is not evident anywhere as you ride past, just a small wooden service station among the gum trees. The bare worked-over mounds of a mining town appear on the outskirts of Southern Cross. This little town, where the streets are named after constellations, marks the start of the WA goldfields. A mine the locals call "The Golden Pig" is on the town's doorstep and is a principal employer. Southern Cross became a bustling town when gold was discovered here in 1887. But when bigger and better finds were made at Coolgardie and Kalgoorlie a few years later, a major exodus occurred and the town became a mere stopping point for most miners heading east. There is a tourist information centre here and a small heritage museum. The town also services the surrounding farming district and is the last place with more than one shop before Coolgardie over 180km away.

10km past Southern Cross the landscape changes. The ploughed fields revert back to a sandy plain covered with scraggly mallee (stunted eucalypts), and the highway becomes like a ruler across the semi-desert.

The Yellowdine roadhouse has a diner, cabins and a camping area (which is little more than a clearing in the gum trees behind the petrol tanks). Throughout the night you'll hear distant rumbles build to a rocket-like roar, as trucks barrel by on the highway - the ground trembles and a curious clanging of chains and rattling of metal rises above the crescendo as they missile past.

Australian Beer

A disturbing feature of Australian rural roads is the considerable collection of discarded beer cans, which line the roadside. The cans say something about the Aussie attitude to drinking and driving, but they're also an insight into the parochial drinking habits of the locals. Dropped at random into rural Australia, it would be easy to identify which state you were in by a quick check of the roadside beer cans; in WA "Swan Larger", in Qld. "XXXX", in Vic. "VB", in NSW "Fosters", etc.

Up until the mid-1980's Australia's 17 million hectolitre-a-year brewing industry was split strongly along state lines. But by the late-1990's take-overs and buy-outs saw the market dominated by two brewing giants; Lion Nathan (a New Zealand company run by that country's richest man) and Foster's Brewing Group, although the locally favoured brand names were often retained. In addition to their own preferred beers, each state uses its own terminology for glass sizes. A 285ml drink in WA is a glass, in SA a schooner, in Vic. a pot, in NSW a middy, and so on. As a result an out-of-stater is easily recognised when he asks for a beer by the wrong glass name.

Lion Nathan caused a ruckus in brewing circles in late 1995 when one of its subsidiaries, the SA Brewing Company, released a beer named "Duff". Twentieth Century Fox, the distributors of the TV show "The Simpsons", in which Homer slurps Duff beers, sued the brewer over their use of the name. In his ruling Judge Brian

1851 February 6 is Black Thursday a day of terrible bush fires around Melbourne. Ash is blown as far as Tasmania

Tamberlin, who spent time watching The Simpsons and reviewing the beer as part of the proceedings, found that under the Trade Practices Act the brewer had illegally exploited the strong association with The Simpsons by making and selling Duff Beer. The SA Brewing Company was forced to halt production, and six-packs of the banned beer, which originally sold for $15, became collectors items advertised for sale at $750.

It's no small exaggeration to say that Australians like their beers (generally pilseners served chilled). The country ranks high on the list of beer consumption per capita, and Australia's Northern Territory reportedly has the worlds heaviest drinkers at an average of about 270 litres/year per person. Even so, the beer companies have had a hard time keeping sales up in recent years, as wine has become fashionable with a traditionally beer-drinking public. The 1970's and 1980's saw wine consumption double, and it continues to grow. The brewers are still in the battle though, pouring advertising dollars into Australia's mainstream male sports in an effort to sustain the image of a play-hard, drink-hard "Ocker" (the type of person that throws their cans out the car window).

Camping:
Southern Cross Caravan Park, Great Eastern Hwy, Southern Cross, Ph (08) 9049 1212, T$6 ▯ Yellowdine Roadhouse, Great Eastern Hwy, Yellowdine, Ph (08) 9024 2001, T$2

Motel/Hotel:
Moorine Rock Motor Hotel, Great Eastern Hwy, Moorine Rock, Ph (08) 9049 1235, S$40, D$50 ▯ Club Hotel, Antares St, Southern Cross, Ph (08) 9049

1202, S$25, D$40 ▯ The Southern Cross Motel, Canopus St, Southern Cross, Ph (08) 9049 1144, S$48, D$60 ▯ Yellowdine Roadhouse, Great Eastern Hwy, Yellowdine, Ph (08) 9024 2001, S$30, D$40 ▯ Others; Southern Cross

i:
Yilgarn Tourist Information Centre, Great Eastern Highway, Southern Cross, Ph (08) 9049 1001

400km 8km before Southern Cross

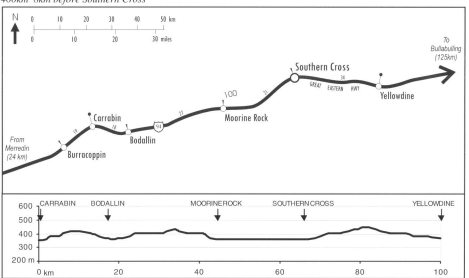

1854 Goldminers in Vic. burn their mining licenses and form the Eureka stockade. Soldiers crush the rebellion killing 22

43

5 YELLOWDINE TO COOLGARDIE

Yellowdine to:

Bullabulling	125km
Coolgardie	154km c, h, m/h, i

Heading east from Yellowdine the Great Eastern Highway rolls gently upward to Coolgardie. There are no farms or houses along the 125km to Bullabulling, and the low scrub covered plain, occasionally dotted with gum trees, stretches to the horizon in every direction. The scrub is home to a diverse set of wildlife including emus, wombats and kangaroos, and regrettably there is road-kill. Often you'll smell the stale odour of a dead animal before you see it - a sad bundle of fur at the end of a violent red swath. As you ride past, a blanket of flies gracefully lifts then settles. In stark contrast, occasional puffs of breeze bring delicate fragrances from unseen wildflowers.

Emus are sometimes visible from the road. These birds are the second largest in the world behind ostriches and are particularly inquisitive in nature. They feature on every Australian bank note, along with the kangaroo, as part of Australia's coat of arms. 60km after leaving Yellowdine, and almost exactly 500km from Fremantle, is a telecommunications tower - the only man-made feature visible for kilometres around apart from the road, the water pipeline, and a string of old telegraph poles.

The Bullabulling pub appears out of the shimmering haze after 125km like a scene from a beer commercial. The pub is cool and dark, and has an atmosphere that suggests pool ques are regularly snapped over heads. It also has a good selection of ice creams.

30km further on is Coolgardie with a main street wide enough to turn a camel train - which is what they did in the old days. Coolgardie's glory days were the 1890's when the discovery of gold caused the population to explode to 15,000. Today the town is a shadow of its former self. Many solid buildings still remain, but the wooden ones in-between have mostly gone, leaving a main street that looks like a toothless grin. The Railway Lodge is one of the few original hotels that has survived, and for $25 you can sleep under the same high ceilings as those doing business during the gold rush did. Across the road at the Denver City Pub a typical Australian scene is played out as the sun sinks; dusty utes with sleepy dogs tied on the back are parked up outside, while inside it's the pokies, sports TV, and beer flowing into the night. Coolgardie has a good historical museum in the Old Courthouse on Bayley St (open daily 9:00am to 5:00pm) and there are markers set around town explaining its history. The town comes alive again every September on Coolgardie Day, which includes among other things camel races.

WA's Eastern Goldfields

Coolgardie sits atop some of the oldest rocks in the world - formed during a distant and poorly understood geologic era known simply as The Archaean. These ancient rocks are part of the Yilgarn Shield, which cuts a broad brush across the lower left quarter of WA. Within the Shield are Greenstone Belts, which hold much of the mineral wealth that has seen WA grow rich. Named because of the green tinged mineral chlorite, these rocks started out life as slices of sea floor until they were squeezed upward between proto-continents jockeying for position on the Earth's surface. During this disruption the rocks were drastically faulted and folded under intense pressures which caused the gold they contained to become concentrated along steeply dipping shears and fractures. Once on the ground surface weathering and erosion took over and started to winnow out the gold.

Alluvial gold was discovered about 3km from Coolgardie in 1892, and the biggest gold rush in Australian history followed. In June 1893 three Irish prospectors, Paddy Hannan, Dan Shea, and Tom Flanagan stumbled onto an even richer strike just east of

1856 Australia is the first country to use a voting system incorporating government printed and distributed ballot papers and supervised secret voting

where Kalgoorlie's main street now is. They rode into Coolgardie 3 days later with 64kg of gold and sparked a new rush east. Hannan and his mates never found the actual source of the Kalgoorlie gold which lay locked in the greenstone 5km south - in a geologic structure 5km long and 1km wide that has become known as "The Golden Mile".

The rush for gold saw 20 hotels spring up in Coolgardie and 90 in Kalgoorlie. They catered to the miners and to rich investors visiting from the eastern colonies and London. When gold prices eventually dropped many closed and today most are gone. By the 1930's mining had virtually ceased at Coolgardie. In the 1960's Kalgoorlie's future looked unsure too but a nickel find at Kambalda and a jump in gold prices saved it.

About 1,500 tons of gold has been mined at Kalgoorlie (that's a cube of gold 4.3m x 4.3m x 4.3m, or about 1% of world production to date). But without the backing of big business Hannan and his mates never became seriously wealthy - Hannan died in Adelaide in 1925 on a government pension and the other two died penniless.

Camping:
Coolgardie Caravan Park, 99 Bayley St, Coolgardie, Ph (08) 9026 6009, T$14 ☐ The Haven Caravan Park, Great Eastern Hwy, Coolgardie, Ph (08) 9026 6123, T$8

Hostel:
Railway Lodge, 75 Bayley St, Coolgardie, Ph (08) 9026 6238, S$25, D$35 ☐

Motel/Hotel:
Denver City Hotel, 73 Bayley St, Coolgardie, Ph (08) 9026 6031, S$25, D$45 ☐ Caltex Coolgardie Motel, 110 Bayley St, Coolgardie, Ph (08) 9026 6049, S$40, D$50 ☐ Others; Coolgardie

i:
Coolgardie Tourist Bureau, 62 Bayley Street, Coolgardie, Ph (08) 9026 6090

Bike Shops:
(Nearest is 38km NE in Kalgoorlie) ☐ Johnston Cycles, 78 Boulder Rd, Kalgoorlie, Ph (08) 9021 1157 ☐ Hannans Cycles, 44 Boulder Rd, Kalgoorlie, Ph (08) 9021 2467

500km 60km past Yellowdine

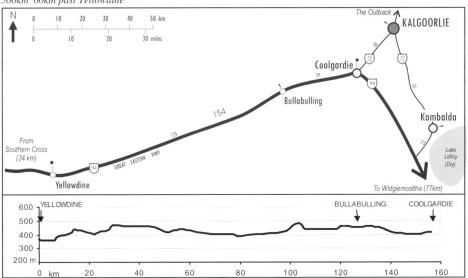

6 COOLGARDIE TO NORSEMAN

Coolgardie to:

Widgiemooltha	77km c, m/h
Norseman	167km c, h, m/h, i

From Coolgardie the road doglegs south and travels more than 160km down the Coolgardie-Esperance Highway to Norseman. The road is mostly flat to gently rolling. The only stop along the way is the roadhouse at Widgiemooltha.

On the outskirts of Coolgardie a few backyard miners still pick over their diggings behind "KEEP OUT" signs. Past these the land looks pretty much untouched. The road is lined by scrub and eucalypts, and roadside markers count down the distance to Norseman in 10km intervals...NO90...NO80...NO70...

77km from Coolgardie is the Widgemooltha service station and roadhouse, which has food, water, and basic accommodation. After Widemooltha it's another 90km unbroken to Norseman. Keep an eye out for giant Wedgetail eagles that can sometimes be seen circling high in the sky in these remote parts. 7km before Norseman the road crosses Lake Cowan, a huge shining salt pan criss-crossed with tyre tracks. At the edge of town is a greeting sign: "Norseman - The Golden Gate To The Western State" and just past this, is the turn off for the Eyre Highway - the start of the Nullarbor crossing. Signs give the distance to Balladonia and Adelaide and warn of "Limited Water Norseman To Ceduna, Obtain Supplies At Norseman". Continue past the Eyre Highway turn-off and straight ahead down Norseman's main street.

Norseman has the tatty look of a mining town in decline. The old wooden buildings have sagging verandas and the newer buildings are cheaply constructed. The image is not helped by the Central Norseman Gold Corporation's enormous tailings dump, which serves as a backdrop for the town. The place has a frontier feel, with travellers arriving and departing on the 1,200km crossing to Ceduna in South Australia. Cars towing caravans and tour buses are parked up outside the motels on the edge of town and the tourists look shell-shocked as they scurry along the dusty streets in their clean clothes. Beacon Hill Lookout, a short walk or ride from the main street, has good views over the town, the salt lakes, and the immense plain stretching eastward.

The Eyre Highway

Norseman is the start of the Eyre Highway and the Nullarbor crossing. Prior to World War II the journey between Norseman and Ceduna was still a momentous undertaking. The dirt track saw little traffic, was rough and dusty, and got bogged down when it rained.

The first travellers across the Nullarbor were Aboriginals, who formed an ancient network of walking paths. Edward John Eyre, the first European to make the crossing, saw their footprints on his expedition in 1841, which followed a route close to the coast.

The first established track ran from Esperance in WA to Fowlers Bay in SA, and was formed by a handful of hardy folk who set out in the 1860's and 1870's to eke out cattle and sheep stations on the Nullarbor. This route was slightly inland from Eyre's and was also used as a supply line during the construction of the Overland Telegraph between Adelaide and Perth. In the early 1890's miners headed west along this track, before turning north up a path called Dempster's Track (named after the first settlers at Fraser Range) to the goldfields at Coolgardie and Kalgoorlie. As Norseman grew into a sizeable stop, the miners shortened their route by skipping Esperance and making directly for Coolgardie via Norseman.

Little was done to this track in the following years - until the Japanese bombed Darwin in February 1942. Fearing an invasion from the north the Government initiated an urgent upgrade of the Nullarbor track between Norseman and Penong. Under the direction of the Army over 1,000 men from the Main Roads Department of WA, and the Highway Department of SA, worked on their respective sides of the road. Using what machinery was available, supplemented by picks and shovels, they created an 8.5m wide, 1,150km long, gravel road, which became the Eyre Highway. The only sealed strips were the brief descents onto the Roe Plain at Madura and Eucla.

Of course the invasion never happened, and for a long time after the war the average number of cars making the crossing was less than one a day. Eventually traffic increased and bitumen sealing started sporadically from either end. The joining of the asphalt finally took place in October 1969, at a spot marked by a plaque on the climb up Eucla Pass.

Camping:
Widgiemooltha Pub & Roadhouse, Esperance Hwy, Widgiemooltha, Ph (08) 9020 8030, T$8 □ Gateway Caravan Park, Cnr Prinsep & McIvor St, Norseman, Ph (08) 9039 1500, T$11

Hostel:
Lodge 101 Guest House, 101 Princep St, Norseman, Ph (08) 9039 1541, Dm$25

Motel/Hotel:
Widgiemooltha Pub & Roadhouse, Esperance Hwy, Widgiemooltha, Ph (08) 9020 8030, S$35, D$35 □ Railway Hotel-Motel, 106 Roberts St, Norseman, Ph

(08) 9039 1115, S$40, D$60 □ Great Western Motel, Cnr Prinsep & McIvor St, Norseman, Ph (08) 9039 1633, S$60, D$71 □ Norseman Eyre Motel, Cnr Eyre & Esperance Hwys, Norseman, Ph (08) 9039 1130, S$69, D$76 □ Others; Norseman

i:
Norseman Tourist Bureau, Roberts St, Norseman, Ph (08) 9039 1071

Bike Shop:
No bike shops but Mitre 10, a hardware store on Roberts St in Norseman, has some bicycle parts.

600km 1km past Coolgardie

700km 65km before Norseman

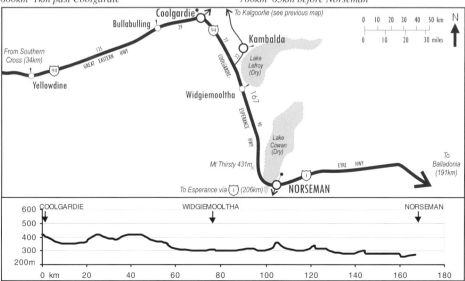

NORSEMAN

Norseman is a gold mining town on the verge of the Outback - the last major town before Ceduna 1,200km to the east in SA. Norseman doesn't really have any attractions that would warrant a visit in itself, but it is a good place to rest before, or after, tackling the Nullarbor.

The town's population is around 1,800 and many of these work for the town's mine or mine supporting industries. Highway 94 from Coolgardie runs right into Norseman, becoming Prinsep Street, before running out the other end as Highway 1 to Esperance. Most amenities are on Prinsep or Roberts St's.

The **Tourist Bureau** is on the corner of Sinclair and Roberts St's and next door is the town **swimming pool**. Also in Roberts St is a statue of a horse with no rider honouring **"Norseman"** - a diggers nag that apparently kicked up the gold nugget which lead to the town's establishment.

Across the rail line from the pool, on the corner of Battery and Mines Rd's is the **Historical and Geological Collection** with exhibits from the Gold Rush and early settler periods. Continue up Mines Rd to the **Beacon Hill Lookout** for 360° views of the surrounding salt lakes. On the way you'll pass between the huge eroding **slime dumps** of the Central Norseman Gold Company. Tours of this massive open cut mine are available - check with the Tourist Bureau. The road to the lookout also passes the **Bullen Decline**, an underground operation reputedly mining the richest quartz reef in Australia.

Nearby, **Dundas Hills** and **Lake Dundas** (the original town site with a lone grave on the lake-edge) are popular picnic spots. The Tourist Bureau also sells fossicking permits for **Gemstone Lease**, an area with opalite, jasper, and agate.

One thing you may want to take advantage of in Norseman is the town swimming pool, heading eastward it's the last one for a long time.

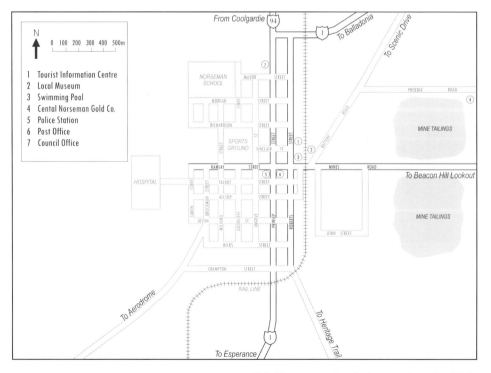

1868 The transportation of prisoners to Australia officially ends

ALTERNATIVE: SOUTHERN LOOP

If the prospect of crossing the Nullarbor is too daunting, head south past Norseman to the beautiful beaches around Esperance. At the end of the nineteenth century Esperance was a busy port servicing WA's Eastern Goldfields. Today it's a centre for the surrounding farming district. Edward Eyre was the first white man to pass through the Esperance area, near the end of his Nullarbor crossing in 1841.

The highway west from Esperance passes near the Stokes and Fitzgerald River National Parks, which preserve some of the prettiest stretches of coastline in Western Australia, before reaching Albany - the first town to be settled in WA (1826). Albany was also the location for Australia's last mainland whaling station, which closed in 1978.

The South Coast Highway runs near a superb coastline between Albany and Walpole. 6.5km out of the village of Nornalup (an interestingly named spot meaning "meeting place of the yellow-bellied snake" in Aboriginal) is the "Valley of the Giants" with Tingle and Karri forests containing some of Australia's tallest trees. Karri is a gum (a sub-group within eucalypts) that thrives around wet coastal areas. These trees grow so high that huts in their tops are used as fire lookouts. After Walpole the South Western Highway heads across country to Bunbury, the third largest town in WA, with a thriving timber industry and tourist trade. Highway 1 north follows the Old Coast Road to Perth past the Yalgorup National Park. Possible stages for this route are:

Norseman to Salmon Gums (98km) ▢ Salmon Gums to Esperance (108km) ▢ Esperance to Ravensthorpe (187km) ▢ Ravensthorpe to Jerramungup (114km) ▢ Jerramungup to Albany (177km) ▢ Albany to Walpole (120km) ▢ Walpole to Manjimup (119km) ▢ Manjimup to Bunbury (131km) ▢ Bunbury to Mandurah (102km) ▢ Mandurah to Perth (77km)

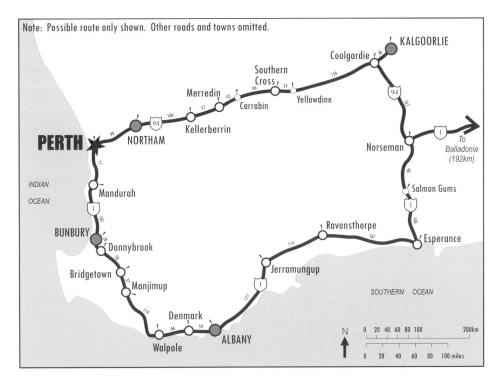

7 NORSEMAN TO BALLADONIA

Norseman to:
Balladonia   192km c, h, m/h

Leaving Norseman east bound is the start of the Eyre Highway and what is loosely referred to as the Nullarbor crossing. Actually, the road touches the true treeless Nullarbor Plain for only a few kilometres near Nullarbor itself in SA, but the trip between Norseman and Ceduna is still considered by most Australians as "crossing the Nullarbor". The majority of drivers describe this trip as immeasurably tedious, a necessary obstacle in driving to, or from, the West Coast, but at the slower pace of a bicycle the areas fascinating wildlife and hard won history are easier to appreciate, and the Nullarbor trek becomes truly memorable.

The 192km between Norseman and Balladonia make this the longest unsupported distance on the tour. There are no facilities between these two settlements. If this distance is too much for you to cycle in a day you will have to free camp just off the road, or make other arrangements to get to Balladonia.

As the signs leaving Norseman remind you, there is limited water between Norseman and Ceduna. Water is available at the service stations and roadhouses along the way but you may be expected to pay for it. There are a few public water tanks on the Nullarbor crossing that collect rainwater, but these should not be relied on because of vandalism. Leaving Norseman make sure you have enough water and food for the journey to Balladonia.

On the south side of the highway a few kilometres out from Norseman is Mt Jamberlain, one of the oldest rock formations in Australia, dating from the early Archean (i.e. a couple of billion years ago).

The road to Balladonia is gently rolling and there is a noticeable reduction in the amount of traffic compared to the Perth to Coolgardie leg. Roadworks were recently completed on this stretch, and there is a wide shoulder leading out of Norseman.

Initially the route consists of long straights gently rolling over scrub and patchy eucalypt country - the horizon broken only by occasional rounded rock outcrops. In places the bush is blackened by fire and "No Fire" signs are conspicuous at the rest stops.

About 100km from Norseman, the road gradually crests the Fraser Range, passing through charming grassy meadows framed with rock outcrops and trees, before gradually dropping back onto the ubiquitous saltbush and mallee scrub plain that dominates much of the Nullarbor trip.

The Balladonia roadhouse has a service station and shop, hotel and motel facilities, dormitory accommodation, a camping area, and a restaurant.

Skylab

America's first space station - Skylab - dropped out of the sky near Balladonia on 11 July 1979.

The American's had spent the early part of the 1970's figuring out what to do with the Apollo rockets after the moon landings. They came up with the idea of leaving some of the liquid hydrogen out of the huge Saturn V rocket and building a space station inside instead. The plan called for the rocket to split apart after leaving the Earth's atmosphere and deliver Skylab nicely into orbit. At the 1973 launch, however, a major malfunction occurred when a meteorite shield accidentally deployed and was ripped off along with half the solar panels used to power the station.

Eleven days later a crew was sent up (with bolt cutters on an 8-meter pole) to repair the damage, which they eventually did, and Skylab became an orbiting laboratory.

1870 John Forrest leads an expedition from Perth to Adelaide, the journey takes 6 months

One of the main functions of the station was to observe the Sun, which ironically was to be the celestial body that caused Skylab's premature demise. An increase in Sun spot activity on the Sun's surface caused the Earth's atmosphere to fractionally expand, enough to cause drag on Skylab's low orbit and gradually pull the station back to Earth.

NASA, shifting uncomfortably in their seats, couldn't predict exactly where the 85,000kg station would land, and after 34,981 orbits Skylab plummeted out of the sky on a quiet Nullarbor night.

One local said "I could hear the pieces windmilling through the air, the animals were running all over the place, the dogs were barking and the horses were galloping around the paddock". The people who saw Skylab burn up on re-entry described a brilliant ball of fire, changing from bright blue to orange red, and leaving a long glowing smoke trail.

Pieces of Skylab, along with a collection of other space junk off the Nullarbor, are on display in the excellent little museum in Ceduna.

It would be a loss if you can't make it to the Ceduna museum, but if you want to see pieces of Skylab there are other places to go. For example, a tiny fragment is on display at the Griffith Observatory in Los Angeles.

Camping:
Balladonia Caravan Facility, Eyre Hwy, <u>Balladonia</u>, Ph (08) 9039 3453, T$6

Motel/Hotel:
Balladonia Motel Hotel, Eyre Hwy, <u>Balladonia</u>, Ph (08) 9039 3453, S$69, D$86

Hostel:
Balladonia Roadhouse Hostel, Eyre Hwy, <u>Balladonia</u>, Ph (08) 9039 3453, Dm$17

800km 30km past Norseman

900km 65km before Balladonia

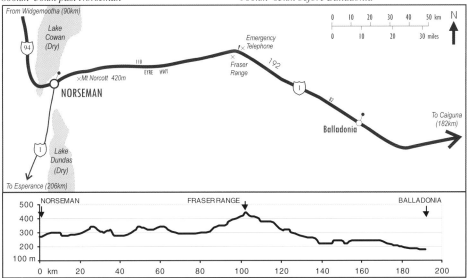

1872 An overland telegraph connecting Adelaide and Darwin operates for the first time

Balladonia to:
Caiguna   182km c, m/h

Balladonia to Caiguna is another very long stretch with no facilities en route, so be sure to carry enough food and water. There are two public water tanks along this section but because of the possibility of interference, these they should not be relied on.

Soon after leaving Balladonia the road becomes pancake flat, with only the faintest rises and falls, and even the scrub and eucalypts seem to thin out. About 34km past Balladonia a sign declares "90 Mile Straight - Australia's Longest Straight Road 146.6km". This is a somewhat modest claim because the straight is generally regarded as the longest stretch of straight sealed road in the world (the road's twin is the longest stretch of straight rail in the world on the Trans-Continental Railway to the north near the WA/SA border). The road is so flat in places that it stretches ahead to a pinprick on the horizon until the Earth's curvature causes it to drop out of sight. It's a glorious ride in a tailwind - or a cycling nightmare in a headwind.

The plain itself started life as an ancient seafloor. Marine life that lived in a primordial sea, which extended far inland at one time, died and collected on the ocean floor before being compacted, cemented, then uplifted 10 million years ago and eroded. The result is an immense flat, the largest limestone plain in the world, dotted with sinkholes and caverns. There is reportedly an impressive blowhole about 5km west of Caiguna, only 10m from the road, unfortunately it's not signposted, and without local help, you're unlikely to find it. Subterranean winds and drafts move in and out of these blowholes and old photographs show Victorian ladies holding their handkerchiefs over them with the hankies blowing straight up.

Roadside markers tick off the distance to Caiguna at 10km intervals, and near the last one of these is a sign reminding you how big Australia is by instructing travellers to turn their watches forward 45 minutes.

After 90 straight miles there is the novelty of a bend in the highway. On the bend is the Caiguna roadhouse, with the standard roadhouse amenities. This roadhouse is a popular stopping point for truckies. They roll up in trucks adorned with crude names and climb out, like soft winkles prized from their shells, wearing the truck drivers standard uniform of tight shorts, singlets and flip-flops. They fill up on free coffee, offered at the roadhouses to keep them awake, climb back in their rigs, and drive away.

25km south of Caiguna is a memorial to John Baxter, a companion of Edward Eyre on that first Nullarbor crossing. Baxter never made it past here though, he was murdered by two of the Aborigines in their party who ran off with all the food they could carry. The ground was too hard for Eyre to even bury his friend. Sheer cliffs that run for almost 200km along the southern coast here have been named in Baxter's honour.

Arthur Richardson

Arthur Richardson probably passed near the site of the Caiguna roadhouse in 1896 during his crossing of the Nullarbor - the first by bicycle. Richardson, the son of a Kalgoorlie doctor, was a wanderlust traveller who would think nothing of walking hours alone in Outback Australia to visit friends. In 1896, he set off from Coolgardie on a single speed clunker and rode the unformed track to Adelaide in 31 days. He must have enjoyed the experience because three years later he set off from Perth and became the first to pedal around Australia, taking 243 days - an impressive feat at a time when gravel roads, if any, were the norm.

1877 An overland telegraph connecting Adelaide and Perth is completed

Jim Fitzpatrick, in his excellent book "The Bicycle and the Bush", describes cycling in early Australia. At the end of the 19th Century camels and bicycles were the two principal modes of Outback travel in WA, and the faster of the two was usually the bicycle. Migrating miners, shearers, swagmen, commercial travellers, and clergymen visiting their flocks all used bicycles. Bike riders were employed to patrol the water pipeline to Kalgoorlie and WA's vermin proof fences. Before 1896, when a telegraph line was completed, the quickest way to get a message from Southern Cross to Kalgoorlie was via the cycle express messenger service. The heat and terrain made cycling tough, and often bikes had to be carried over sandy patches. But one break these early riders did get was when they could follow "camel pads". These narrow, smooth pathways were formed by the padded feet of camel trains run by Afghan traders. These trains carried supplies to the remotest Outback settlements and the tracks they followed were by far the preferred cycling surface.

Little is known of Arthur Richardson's life following his cycling days, he reportedly fought in the Boer War, was invalided to England, then served again in World War I. After this he seems to disappear from the pages of Australian history.

An example of the type of bicycle Richardson would have used on these early long distance trips is on display in the transportation section of the Powerhouse Museum in Sydney.

Camping:
Caiguna Roadhouse, Eyre Hwy, Caiguna, Ph (08) 9039 3459, T$8

Motel/Hotel:
John Eyre Motel (Caiguna Roadhouse), Eyre Hwy, Caiguna, Ph (08) 9039 3459, S$72, D$83

1000km 35km past Balladonia

1100km 45km before Caiguna

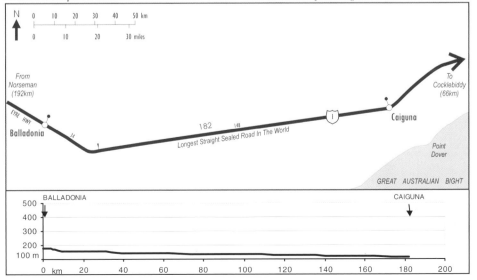

1880 Ned Kelly, surrounded by police, wears a home made suit of armour and comes out firing. He is wounded and later hung

Caiguna to:

Cocklebiddy	66km c, m/h
Madura	158km c, m/h

Continuing east from Caiguna to Madura, the highway is basically flat. The only exception is a brief but steep descent as the road drops off the Hampton Tablelands onto the coastal plain at Madura. There is the opportunity for a shorter day's ride by staying at Cocklebiddy - 66km from Caiguna.

Leaving Caiguna the road continues through a largely untouched wilderness where groups of kangaroos can often be seen bounding across the plain between the stunted eucalypts. Cocklebiddy Cave is located along this stretch, in the barrens to the north of the road.

The area around Cocklebiddy is part of the Nuytsland Nature Reserve, which stretches south to the Great Australian Bight and extends for hundreds of kilometres along the remote coastline. The Eyre Bird Observatory is about 50km from Cocklebiddy, most of it along a rugged 4WD track. Accommodation is available, however, visits need to be arranged in advance. The observatory is located in an original Nullarbor Telegraph Station built in 1897 and restored in 1977. It's about 1km from the ocean and is near a spot called "The Sandpatch" where Edward Eyre discovered water on his 1841 overland trek to Albany. Eyre and his party camped at The Sandpatch for 4 weeks after finding fresh water soaks below depressions in the sand dunes. It was soon after leaving this spot that Eyre's expedition met with tragedy when his companion John Baxter was murdered.

The Cocklebiddy roadhouse has fuel, food, water, and accommodation. Hanging on the roadhouse wall is a roughly made cricket bat. The bat was used in a game between stranded truckers and motorists, a while back, when flooding blocked the highway for several days - a reminder that when it eventually rains out here it can rain a lot.

Back on the road this is the heart of the Nullarbor. Stub-tailed lizards soak up the sun and black crows, with squawks like bleating lambs, wait to peck the eyes out of anything that gets run over. The flies are ever present, gathering whenever you stop or ride slower than about 15km/hr, and a conscious effort has to be made not to weave along the road while swatting at them.

About 2km from Madura the road suddenly and unexpectedly reaches the edge of an escarpment and the highway drops down Madura Pass onto the Roe Plain. From the top of the Pass the view is of another endless plain, dotted with mallee and saltbush, and a long straight road stretching east. The trip down the Pass provides a cross-section of the plain - fossilised oysters, small bivalves, and gastropods are exposed in the road cut and it's a chance to have a close look at the same sheer cliffs that front the Southern Ocean east of Eucla.

Madura station started as a pastoral lease taken up in 1876. At one time cavalry horses and polo ponies for the British Army in India were bred here. The Madura Pass Oasis Motel is near the base of the cliffs and is one of the more luxurious Nullarbor roadhouses. The campground however is as barren as the other stops and has a noisy generator located too close to the camping area.

The Royal Flying Doctor Service

Just east of Madura a sign warns motorists to watch out for aircraft occasionally landing on the highway. In emergencies the Royal Flying Doctor Service uses the road here to fly in help, and fly out patients who would otherwise face a lengthy road trip.

The service was founded in 1928 by a Presbyterian minister, John Flynn, who after

1885 Tom Roberts establishes the "Heidelberg School" of painting with his unique Australian bush scenes

working in the isolation of Outback Qld., had set up teams of "boundary riders" (Reverends on camel- and horse-back who ministered to massive parishes). In 1917 Flynn received a letter from a young Australian pilot on the way to World War I, suggesting the new technology of aeroplanes would be ideal for covering the large Outback distances in emergencies. The young pilot, Clifford Peel, died in France during the last months of the war but the seed of the idea stuck with Flynn. The problem was how to summon help from the middle of a continent covering over 7,500,000km^2. Enter Alfred Traeger, an Adelaide engineer and radio buff. Working with Flynn, Traeger (who was obviously not bound by conventional thinking) developed a pedal powered wireless that could be used in the Outback to call for help. In 1928, Flynn's dream of a flying doctor service went into operation with a single plane leased from the fledgling airline Qantas. The scheme was a big success, and has provided essential services ever since.

In 1996, the Royal Flying Doctor Service undertook 14,000 evacuations, conducted 4,500 remote health care clinics, and averaged 82 flights a day all around Australia. The service has become a source of national pride, even spawning a dramatised TV series, and the Reverend Flynn's portrait is on the $20 note.

Camping:
Cocklebiddy Roadhouse, Eyre Hwy, Cocklebiddy, Ph (08) 9039 3462, T$8 ☐ Madura Roadhouse, Eyre Hwy, Madura, Ph (08) 9039 3464, T$10

Motel/Hotel:
Eyre Bird Observatory, Eyre Hwy, S of Cocklebiddy*, Ph (08) 9039 3450, Fax (08) 9039 3440, S$50-70 (bookings essential) *Access via 50km off-road track ☐ Wedgetail Inn (Cocklebiddy Roadhouse), Eyre Hwy, Cocklebiddy, Ph (08) 9039 3462, S$58, D$66 ☐ Madura Pass Oasis Motel (Madura Roadhouse), Eyre Hwy, Madura, Ph (08) 9039 3464, S$52-65, D$52-80

1200km 15km before Cocklebiddy   *1300km 5km before Madura*

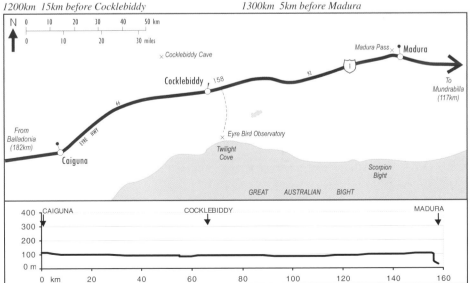

10 MADURA TO MUNDRABILLA

Madura to:

Mundrabilla   117km c, m/h

The highway between Madura and Mundrabilla is flat. The road follows the base of the Hampton Tablelands escarpment until a signposted outcrop called Moodini Rocks, where it heads out across the plain, leaving behind the pretty scrub of the escarpment and traversing a mallee and saltbush plain.

Mundrabilla Station, an incredibly remote spot, was one of the first stations on the Nullarbor. It was settled back in 1871 when the leaseholders walked out to their new home (you can imagine their impressions on the trip out and when they arrived).

This stretch of highway entered local folklore in January 1988 when a woman named Faye Knowles reported to Police she was driving eastward near Mundrabilla with her three kids, when they saw a light hovering over the road ahead of them. As they approached the eggcup shaped light apparently sped towards them then hovered directly above their car as they tried to out-run it. The next thing they knew all four tires lost touch with the road and the car reportedly lifted off the Highway. They smelt a burning odour and the car filled with smoke before they were dropped back onto the highway - blowing a tire. The Knowles apparently jumped out and ran into the bushes to hide, eventually emerging to change tires and drive on to Mundrabilla to tell their story.

Slightly more verifiable evidence for flying objects from outer space was discovered near here in 1966, when a geologist unearthed the Mundrabilla meteorite - Australia's largest at 11 tonnes.

The Mundrabilla roadhouse is one of the smaller roadhouses. It has a service station, box-style cabins, a camping patch, and a diner that serves good meals. The service station looks like any other with its large "Caltex" sign flickering above the forecourt, but sitting out here on the uninhabited plain by itself, it has the feel of a space station rather than a service station.

Behind the roadhouse is a mini-zoo with a goat, emus, peacocks, some sad-looking parrots, and Carmel the Camel - a plaque on the enclosure indicating she was found by the Trans-Continental rail line in 1979 next to her dead mother.

Australia's Camels

Australia is the only place in the world you are likely to see road signs warning of wild camels. That's because no where else in the world has wild herds anymore. The Australian beasts are the ancestors of camels that were used to explore and open up the country's Outback areas and were then set free after road and rail systems were built.

In June 1860, George Landis and John King bought the first camels into Australia. Acting under instructions from the Victorian Expedition Committee, they sourced 24 camels from Afghanistan, along with 3 Afghan handlers to control the unruly beasts. They walked the camels back to Karachi in India and loaded them on a boat bound for Melbourne. At Melbourne wharf the animals were unloaded, much to the curiosity of the locals, and marched to Parliament House where they were installed in the stables. The camels proved their suitability to the Australian desert during the 1860 Burke and Wills Expedition (in which John King played a major role), and six years later 120 more animals were imported.

During the late 1800's and early 1900's camel trains led by their Afghan handlers were used extensively for inland travel and supplying remote settlements, including the repeater stations on the telegraph line across the Nullarbor.

1888 Gold is found at Southern Cross in WA, then at Coolgardie (1892) and Kalgoorlie (1893)

The Afghan and Indian camel drivers (collectively known as "Afghans") typically came to Australia as contract workers to provide handling services for pastoralists wanting to extend their holdings, or for expeditions requiring camels. Many stayed on after their contracts were up and established their own camel trains, sometimes supplementing them with horses and oxen. Horses were used for Outback travel when feed was available but the camels big advantage was that during the dry season they would eat mulga (a desert species of acacia), while horses would not. In flat country supplies could be towed behind the camels in wagons, but in rough country the supplies had to be strapped to the sides of the animals.

The Afghans relations with other settlers were generally cordial but cool, and most lived in "Ghan towns" on the fringes of Outback settlements. (Afghan Rock near Balladonia is reportedly named after an Afghan who was murdered there in a dispute over a water hole).

By the 1930's camel trains had almost completely been replaced by motorised transport, and the Afghans seem to have melted into the population or left for home. The contribution that the Afghans and their camel trains made to the exploration and development of Australia has been remembered in the naming of the Adelaide to Darwin train - The Ghan.

Camping:
Mundrabilla Roadhouse, Eyre Hwy, <u>Mundrabilla</u>, Ph (08) 9039 3465, T$6

Motel/Hotel:
Mundrabilla Motor Hotel, Eyre Hwy, <u>Mundrabilla</u>, Ph (08) 9039 3465, S$50, D$60

1400km 15km before Mundrabilla

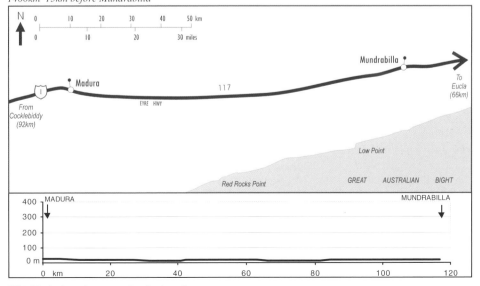

Mundrabilla to:

Eucla	66km	c, m/h
Border Village	78km	c, m/h

This is one of the shorter stages on the Nullarbor. The 78km between Mundrabilla and Border Village in SA are flat except for a short climb at Eucla back onto the Hampton Tablelands. Leaving Mundrabilla the road crosses the last of the Roe Plain, barren except for knee high scrub. 20km before Eucla, what looks like a dust storm on the horizon appears - it is actually the sand dunes marking the foot of Eucla Pass. At the top of the Pass is a monument to Edward Eyre overlooking the plain he once traversed, and a traditional Lithuanian cross for the protection of travellers, erected by the owner of the Eucla Motel. Eucla itself looks over a majestic blue sweep of the Southern Ocean.

The settlement is the one of the oldest on the Nullarbor and is a fascinating place. In the late 19th Century, an ambitious project was launched to build a telegraph link between the completely isolated west and the seat of authority in the east. Construction teams set out from both ends and after many difficulties the link between Perth and Adelaide was made in 1877. Part of the line was a repeater station built at Eucla, which employed up to 40 men to relay messages. A team of SA telegraphists transcribed the incoming Morse messages and passed them across a dividing table to the WA team, which re-tapped them westward. The actual line was a single iron wire, selected in favour of copper because it sagged less and required fewer support poles.

The line was, in the Australian vernacular - a bugger to maintain. Often sand drifts would engulf the poles, eventually reaching the crossbar and breaking the wire, at other times sea spray would affect the line resulting in the interruption of transmission. After the Trans-Continental rail line was completed the telegraph line was relocated to the north and the community which had grown around the Eucla station faded. Shifting sands are now slowly engulfing the old stone telegraph building and only the chimneys and tops of the walls are visible. The original town site is a few kilometres down a gravel road on the coast, along with the remnants of a jetty once used to unload cargo.

Present day Eucla is the biggest of the Nullarbor settlements with a large motel complex, Police and Royal Flying Doctor bases, a small museum, service station, restaurant, and camping facilities. The museum has an interesting collection of photos of Edward Eyre, both young and old, and items from Eucla's glory days.

SA and Border Village are another 12km east, past an agricultural checkpoint. The WA/SA boundary is marked, in true Australian fashion, by a huge fibreglass kangaroo holding out a can of Victoria Bitter. Border Village has none of the nostalgia or charm of Eucla and is particularly dusty and fly ridden even by Nullarbor standards.

Old Eucla

Eucla arose because the telegraph technology of the time required a manual repeating station halfway between Port Augusta in SA and Albany in WA. The area did have a brief prior history; Edward Eyre stopped at a water soak here in 1841, and 29 years later John Forrest, during his overland expedition between Perth and Adelaide, erected a pole here with a copper plate engraved "Western Australia". Seven years after Forrest passed through the telegraph arrived and the first message was repeated at 4:00pm on December 8, 1877.

The town that grew here because of the telegraph initially consisted of a wooden office, several wooden houses built for the senior staff, and tents for the junior staff. The telegraphists lived in this isolation with their families and children were born and raised.

1895 Banjo Paterson's poem "Waltzing Matilda" is set to music and soon becomes the unofficial national anthem

As usual for the Nullarbor, a shortage of water was the main problem. Eyre's soak had limited supplies, and sometimes camel trains had to bring in water from Kalgoorlie. The settlement lived off tinned meat and preserved vegetables, eagerly awaiting overland mail, which came via Aboriginal runner, and the steamer, which arrived every three months from Albany to re-supply the community.

Eucla grew into several short streets and included a store and even a tennis court. At its height the settlement was the busiest telegraph centre outside the capital cities, with much of the traffic concerning the booming goldfields in the west. In 1899, the original wooden telegraph office was re-built in local stone. Old Eucla's shifting sands can be traced back to those first rabbits released by Thomas Austin near Melbourne. In 1895, folk at Eucla were the first in WA to notice the telltale signs of rabbits. What followed was a rippling sea of rabbits flowing westward. Every piece of foliage in and around the town was stripped and eaten, and the ground became riddled with warrens as the wave moved through Eucla. Urgent warnings were tapped westward and when the danger was finally realised construction started on fences to hold back the tide (*see p.40*).

The decline of old Eucla started in 1909 when an automated repeater station replaced many of the telegraphists. In 1929, the line was superseded by one next to the railway in the north, and Eucla was disconnected - the towns' future sealed. Left to the loosened sands, the memories and buildings of old Eulca have now almost disappeared.

Camping:
Eucla Roadhouse, Eyre Hwy, Eucla, Ph (08) 9039 3468, T$4 ◻ Border Village Roadhouse, Eyre Hwy, Border Village, Ph (08) 9039 3474, $T7

Motel/Hotel:
Amber Hotel Motel, Eyre Hwy, Eucla, Ph (08) 9039 3468, S$65, D$75 ◻ Border Village Motel, Eyre Hwy, Border Village, Ph (08) 9039 3474, S$60, D$68

1500km 4km before Border Village

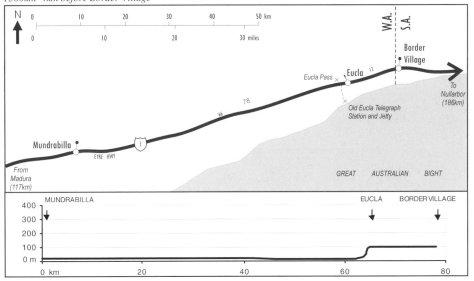

12 BORDER VILLAGE TO NULLARBOR

Border Village to:

Nullarbor   186km c, m/h

Border Village to Nullarbor is another long stretch (186km) with no facilities en route. The road to Nullarbor is ironing board flat, and much of the route runs near the edge of spectacular sheer cliffs dropping straight to the Southern Ocean. A series of lookouts just off the highway take you right to the cliff's edge, which is unfenced and dotted with signs warning about the unstable rim. Between June and October, Southern right whales migrate along the Great Australian Bight and these lookouts are one of the premier whale watching locations in Australia.

The Southern right whale (so called because it was the "right whale" to kill) is making a comeback in these parts after being commercially hunted to the verge of extinction. Almost as soon as Europeans arrived in Australia they started sealing and whaling, and by the early 19th Century whalebone and oil made up over 50% of the export economy. Eyre saw more than 300 French and American whalers during his 1841 expedition along this coast.   By the 1860's, inshore whaling had virtually stopped because they had killed most of the animals. The 1950's, unfortunately, saw a bit of a revival with humpback and sperm whaling being undertaken until the last station near Albany closed in 1978. Today about 500 Southern right whales live in the Southern Ocean off Australia. A number of these migrate each year to the Head of the Bight to breed and give birth. Interestingly, these whales can be easily distinguished by their lack of a dorsal fin.

Leaving Border Village, SA roadside markers start appearing every kilometre and a few kilometres down the road is a much photographed sign warning of camels, wombats, and kangaroos for the next 96km. The roadside vegetation for most of this stretch consists of low mallee, then 1km before the Nullarbor roadhouse a sign identifies the start of the true treeless section of the Nullarbor Plain. The Plain is a carpet of brown grasses and saltbush with hardly any vegetation above knee height. The Eyre Highway only crosses the southern tip of this huge area, which extends inland to the Trans-Continental Railway, and beyond, and covers over 250,000km^2. Much of the true Plain was set aside as the Nullarbor National Park in 1979 (the Park was expanded in 1989 with additional land purchases). Koonanlda Cave, located along this stretch but quite a way north of the road, is the site of an ancient Aboriginal workshop where flint tools were fashioned 80m underground.

The Nullarbor roadhouse, the only one actually on the Nullarbor Plain, has one of the better restaurants between Norseman and Ceduna.

Cocklebiddy Cave

Caves and sinkholes dot the limestone surface of the Nullarbor, leading to a vast subterranean labyrinth. Winds blow in and out some of these holes - to the Aborigines this is the breath of the beast Jeedara who travels underground in tunnels and passages, his lashing tail causing dust storms on the Plain. For prosaic Westerners the caves have been a place to explore and explain, and in 1935 the first speleiological expedition to the Nullarbor was lead by pioneer Australian potholer J. Maitland Thomson.

Cocklebiddy Cave is one of the better-explored caverns. The entrance is a house-sized hole with a rubbly slope leading 90m below the plain. Once underground the cave opens to a cathedral like chamber, complete with a colony of bats in the roof. At the northern end of this chamber is a 200m long lake and at the far end of the lake the roof drops to meet the water.

1901 The Australian Government is established by the formation of The Commonwealth of Australia

In 1972, Phil Prust, Dave Warnes, and Bob Turnball used Scuba gear to dive into this lake for the first time. They swam along a north trending passage, trailing string off a reel behind them. After going 300m, the longest cave dive in Australia at the time, they turned back. In 1983, a French couple entered Cocklebiddy, a few months before a major Australian cave diving effort was scheduled, and reached even further into the unexplored cave. 450m past where the three Australians had turned back the roof again rose out of the water forming a small lake. Continuing on, a rockfall filled the lake and headway was over a jumble of boulders - then another underwater tunnel, this time 2.5km long - before the cave opened into a cavern that was christened Toad Hall.

Only a few divers have ever swum past Toad Hall. Progress in places requires pushing a dive cylinder ahead and then squeezing through after it. In September 1995, Chris Brown, the leader of another Australian team, reached the end of the rope left by the 1983 expedition and attached his own line to continue exploring Cocklebiddy. After 20m the passage narrowed and apparently became impassable and Brown turned around and headed back on the 6km journey to the cave entrance.

Most of the Nullarbor caves are off-limits to casual visitors, and most are hard to find. The Tourist Information Centre in Ceduna has information on tour operators that are permitted to take parties to certain caves.

Camping:
Nullarbor Roadhouse, Eyre Hwy, Nullarbor, Ph (08) 8625 6271, T$8

Motel/Hotel:
Nullarbor Hotel Motel (Nullarbor Roadhouse), Eyre Hwy, Nullarbor, Ph (08) 8625 6271, S$54, D$66

1600km 95km before Nullarbor

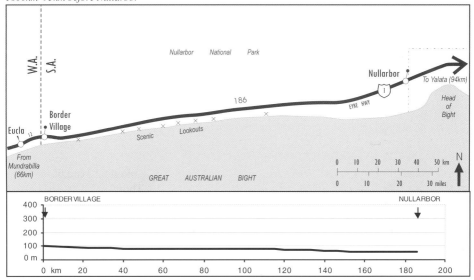

1903 The Coolgardie Water Supply Scheme starts operation

13 NULLARBOR TO NUNDROO

Nullarbor to:
Yalata   94km
Nundroo   145km c, m/h

The Eyre Highway continues across the true Nullarbor Plain for about 20km east of the Nullarbor Roadhouse. Initially the road is flat, then as the highway swings south-east around the Head of the Bight it becomes gently rolling to Nundroo. As the hills become larger the eucalypts get taller and grassy meadows appear, then fields and fences. There is a sense that the epic Nullarbor crossing is nearly over and it is just a matter of time until civilisation reappears.

Australia has the world's greatest array of dry-habitat plants and the highway along this section provides a good sampling, with several vegetation zones; the saltbush of the true Nullarbor Plain, a mixed saltbush and mallee zone, and human influenced pasturelands. Saltbush (low chenopod shrubs) dominates on the limestone Plain where there is little soil development. Unfortunately stock will eat saltbush, and grazing in some areas of the country has lead to the extinction of a number of species. Mallees are ground branching eucalypts, stunted trees that usually form bushes from 3 to 9m tall, typically with leaves only at the ends of branches. There are over 100 mallee species and when conditions are right they form an almost horizontal ground cover. (Mulga, a species of wattle with flattened hairy stems rather than leaves, is another dominant type of ground cover in WA, SA, and NT, and is used by Aborigines for boomerangs)

For most of this stretch the road passes through the Yalata Aboriginal Reserve. There is little to indicate you are on Aboriginal land until a giant boomerang atop the Yalata service station comes into view. The roadhouse sells native arts and crafts, but the place seems to be run by the white folk behind the wide counter. Most of the customers are Aboriginal and there is an awkward meeting of cultures here - a faint tension in the air. Yalata has only basic facilities; a service station and a shop (where you can buy frozen kangaroo tail like baguettes). 2km past the service station is the turnoff to the Yalata Community. Entry is by permit only, and a sign indicates cameras and alcohol are not welcome. Many of the Aborigines at Yalata were relocated here by the Government in the 1950's, in order to keep the area around the Woomera Rocket and Weapon Testing Facility (north of Port Augusta) clear. Prior to moving to Yalata they lived a semi-nomadic lifestyle in the vast areas north of the Trans-Continental rail line.

After Yalata, green fields appear again for the first since Southern Cross in WA. The Nundroo roadhouse has a service station, shop, hotel and motel (with a swimming pool), and a camping area. Watch out for the plastic wrapped buns on the Nundroo shop counter - they may look appealing but check for nibbled edges and mouse sized holes in the wrappers and before consuming.

Edward Eyre

On the coast south of Nundroo is Fowlers Bay. Edward Eyre set out from here in February 1841 to find an overland route to WA. Eyre had previously lead two expeditions into the country north of Adelaide in search of pastoral land before being turned back both times by the barren country (his impressions of the area are reflected in his naming of Mt Hopeless and Mt Deception).

Eyre's small party, consisting of fellow explorer John Baxter, three Aborigines, ten horses, and six sheep left Fowlers Bay in the February heat. From the start a principal problem was a lack of water. Added to this, the dense scrub they encountered forced them to follow the coastline, which had already been charted by Matthew Flinders on his

1906 "The Story of the Kelly Gang", Australia's first feature film, is released

voyage around Australia. The horses often went for days without water and Eyre had to force them not to drink seawater. Things got desperately worse on the night of April 29th. Eyre was tending the horses when he heard a gunshot and returned to find Baxter fatally wounded and two of the Aborigines gone with the almost all the stores. Eyre and the remaining Aborigine, named Wylie, struggled on and were near death when they lucked upon a French whaling ship, which they signalled and obtained provisions from. They resumed their trek and, in a bitter irony, suffered through torrential storms and cold prior to reaching their goal of Albany in WA.

Eyre published an account of his journeys in "Journals of Expeditions of Discovery into Central Australia and Overland from Adelaide to King George's Sound" although many considered his trek to WA to be of little scientific use as it served only to confirm seafarers accounts of this barren coastline.

After his explorations Eyre went on to become a career politician, appointed Protector of Aborigines in Australia, Lieutenant Governor of New Zealand, and then Governor of Jamaica. It was in the Caribbean that Eyre had to deal with another native uprising. His use of force in quelling this revolt lead to 10 years of lingering controversy - one faction strongly critical of Eyre's leadership and another, the Eyre Defence Committee, strongly supportive. The hoopla probably had Eyre wishing for the solitude of the Nullarbor.

Camping:
Nundroo Roadhouse, Eyre Hwy, Nundroo, Ph (08) 8625 6120, T$12

Motel/Hotel:
Nundroo Hotel-Motel (Nundroo Roadhouse), Eyre Hwy, Nundroo, Ph (08) 8625 6120, S$50, D$65

1700km 5km past Nullarbor

1800km 10km past Yalta

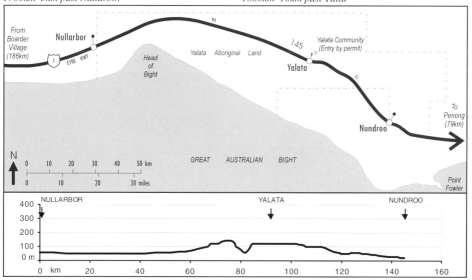

14 NUNDROO TO CEDUNA

Nundroo to:

Bookabie	44km
Penong	79km m/h
Ceduna	152km c, h, m/h, i

From Nundroo to Ceduna the road is gently rolling to rolling and passes through pretty green farmland - a refreshing change from the previous 1,400km.

Bookabie is a tiny settlement; a few houses and an historic schoolhouse ruin. At Penong you can see carloads of surfers heading to Cactus Beach, a point break which receives great waves from the Southern Ocean (although a surfer was recently killed there by a Great White Shark). Penong has several squat solid buildings, including the first grocery store since Norseman. The town has an interesting collection of windmills, which pump the community's water supply. After Penong, the road climbs gently before breaking into rolling hills. 20km before Ceduna the road swings south and the huge grain silos of Thevenard Port become visible. The final barrier to Ceduna is an agricultural checkpoint where inspectors question you about any produce you may have - you'll have to eat any bananas, apples, or other suspect fruit on the spot or give it up.

Ceduna with its Norfolk Island Pines, ocean breezes and sea gulls is a wondrous place after the dusty desert. It has a decent selection of shops (no bicycle shop though) including a bakery on McKenzie St that sells kangaroo pies. Ceduna also has an excellent little museum run by a group of dedicated locals. As well as a good collection of historical exhibits, they have some great "stuff" - the kind of things you only find in small town museums; pieces of NASA's Skylab and crashed Russian satellites collected off the Nullarbor, the container used to transport radioactive material to the Maralinga atomic test site, an enormous stuffed Basking Shark, and an old Ford Consol with a live termite mound under the bonnet.

Australia's Snakes

Australia is unique in that the majority of its snakes are venomous. Of the 121 venomous varieties here, about 12 are seriously dangerous - in fact Australian snakes top the charts for toxicity. The World Health Organisation ranks the potency of snake venoms based on a "lethal dose" test with mice (the amount of venom, mixed into a saline solution, required to kill 50% of mice in a sample is referred to as the "LD50" for a particular species). The lethal dose list is headed by Australia's Inland Taipan (*Oxyuranus microlepidotus*), with an LD50 of 0.025 mg/kg, that's a concentration of one quarter of one tenth of 1 part per million - and the Taipan which grows up to 3m long, is justifiably one of Australia's most feared snakes. Others Australian snakes high in the rankings are the Common Brown (*Pseudonaja textilis*) known as a "town-and-country" snake due to its diverse habitat, and the Peninsula Tiger Snake (*Notechis ater niger*) which is restricted to Kangaroo Is. and other small islands in the Spencer Gulf - a snake rumoured to be the most venomous species in the world for its size.

These alarming statistics are balanced by the fact that the chances of actually being bitten and dying from a snake bite in Australia are probably less than being struck by lightening. The Medical Journal of Australia reported 18 snake bite deaths between 1981 and 1991 (i.e. a lot less than a one-in-a-million chance), whereas snake deaths in Asia or Africa number in the tens of thousand per year. In most of the reported Australian deaths a snake was trodden on or unexpectedly cornered, but a high proportion of the fatalities resulted from bites received while pursuing a snake to kill it.

Interestingly, most snake venoms are not poisonous if swallowed - it's when the

1910 The first powered flight in Australia is made by John Duigan. After seeing photos of the Wright Brothers plane he builds one himself and flies it for just over 7m.

snake's fangs break skin and the venom enters the blood stream that its effects become apparent. Australian snake venoms are predominantly neurotoxins. These work by blocking messages travelling through the nervous system (causing vital functions to shut down), or by firing off nerves repeatedly (causing muscle paralysis). Some venoms are a cocktail of compounds with additional components that cause the victims blood to clot, or blood cells to break down. Fortunately, venom is not always transferred in a snakebite, and it's been suggested that less than half the bites on humans result in effective envenomation (although the Australian Black Snake or mulga (*Pseudechis australis*) has an effective habit of hanging on and chewing). In this respect, the toxicity tests are a misleading gauge of danger - some snakes are retiring and some have restricted ranges. In a nutshell, Australia's high-quality medical facilities and low rural population (most folk are city dwellers) means fatal snakebites are few and far between.

Camping:
Ceduna Caravan & Tourist Centre, McKenzie St, Ceduna, Ph (08) 8625 2150, T$10 ☐ Ceduna Foreshore Caravan Park, South Tce, Ceduna, Ph (08) 8625 2290, T$11 ☐ Ceduna Shelly Beach Caravan Park, Decres Bay Rd, Ceduna, Ph (08) 8625 2012, T$10 ☐ Others; Ceduna

Hostel:
Greenacres Backpackers, 12 Kuhlmann St, Ceduna, Ph (mbl): 0418 811 241, Dm$15

Motel/Hotel:
Penong Hotel, Eyre Hwy, Penong, Ph (08) 8625 1050, S$30, D$40 ☐ Pine Grove Motel, 49 McKenzie St, Ceduna, Ph (08) 8625 2201, S$45, D$50 ☐ Highway 1 Motel, Eyre Hwy, Ceduna, Ph (08) 8625 2208, S$52, D$57 ☐ Others; Ceduna

i:
Ceduna Gateway Tourist Centre, 58 Poynton St, Ceduna, Ph (08) 8625 2780

Bike Shop:
Ceduna's sports goods shop, and hardware store (Mitre 10), have a limited selection of bike parts

1900km 20km before Penong

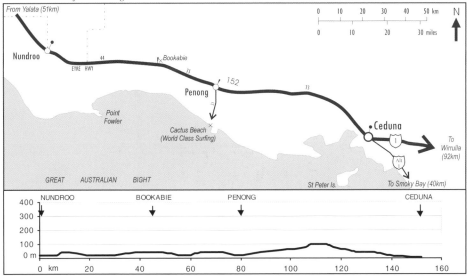

CEDUNA

As the first town of any significance after the Nullarbor Plain, Ceduna is a welcome break. In fact, the town's name is derived from the Aboriginal word "Chedoona", meaning a place to sit down and rest.

On the shores of **Murat Bay** this town of 3,500 looks out to St. Peters Island, the location where, the locals will tell you, Jonathon Swift had Gulliver meeting the tiny Lilliput people on his travels. The centre of Ceduna is the crossroads of **Poynton** and **McKenzie St's**. The town has most things you could want, although it does not have a bike shop. The Mitre 10 hardware store on Poynton Street sells complete bicycles and a few parts, and the sports shop on Poynton St also has some parts. But the nearest decent bike shop is 450km to the east in Port Augusta. The town has a brilliant little **museum**, a **swimming pool**, and an informative **National Parks and Wildlife Service** centre among other things.

Ceduna's **Foreshore Reserve**, with the novelty of grass and trees, is a nice place to rest, or you can fish from the wharf. The clear waters of the Bay offer excellent **fishing** and **diving**, and an **oyster** farming industry has recently been established. From the beach at Ceduna the silos of **Thevenard** are visible 2km away - this deep-sea port ships grain, gypsum, and salt. It also houses a fishing fleet famous for its hauls of King George Whiting and lobster. **Deep sea game fishing** is popular and Ceduna holds the Australian record for the Great White Shark - a 1,200kg monster caught here in 1959 using a 60kg line (a record that will not be broken since Australia has now placed a ban on fishing for the Great White).

Denial Bay, about 12km west of Ceduna, was the original site of the town and there are the ruins of several stone buildings nearby from the days of the early settlers (the spots dourer name came from Matthew Flinders, who was hoping to sail inland here during his 1802 circumnavigation of the continent but was denied a passage).

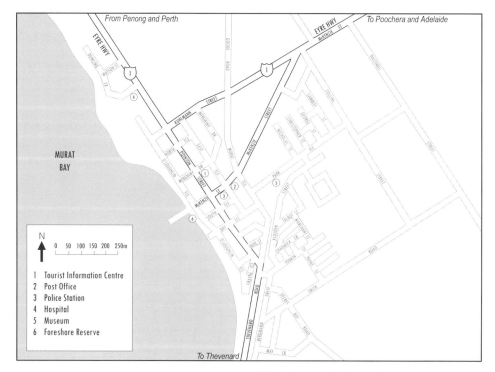

1912 Architect Burley Griffin submits his plan for the layout of Canberra

PORT AUGUSTA

This city of 15,000 regards itself as the gateway to the Australian bush, with the **Finders Ranges** to the north-east and past there, the real **Outback** in almost every direction.

A village was founded here in 1852, after sheep were driven north-east from the Port Lincoln area, and the spot was named after Lady Augusta Young, wife of the fifth Governor of SA. In 1870, the first pole in the Overland Telegraph from Port Augusta to Darwin was planted. The line was completed two years later. In 1875 another pole was planted to start a telegraph line connecting Port Augusta and Perth. This line was also completed in two years.

The **Wadlata Outback Centre** on Flinders Street is the best place to get tourist information on Port Augusta and adventure trips in the area. The centre has numerous hands-on exhibits and audio-visual displays, including a segment on how bicycles helped open up the area in its early days. The **Port Augusta Tourist Information Centre** is also housed here.

Port Augusta's downtown area is focused around **McKay** and **Commercial Streets** where the **Post Office**, **Police Station** and **Town Hall** are located. The **Library** and a **Pioneer Museum** are nearby. The towns **recreation centre** is on Augusta Tce.

The **Royal Flying Doctors** have a regional control centre at Port Augusta, and there is also a **School of the Air** centre, which broadcasts correspondence courses via radio to children living in the Outback. The Tourist Centre has information on tours of these facilities.

To take a break from the bike and see some of the dramatic landscapes around this area consider taking a **4-wheel drive desert tour**, a trip to the natural amphitheatre of **Wilpena Pound** in the Flinders Ranges, visiting the huge **Olympic Dam Mine** at Roxby Downs, or lending a hand on an Outback **cattle and sheep station**. The Tourist Centre has details on all these alternatives.

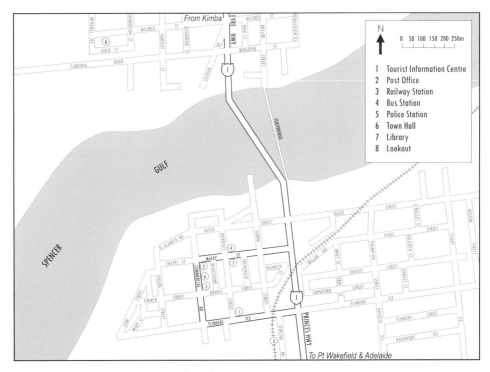

1915 The disastrous ANZAC landings at Gallipoli take place during World War 1

15 CEDUNA TO POOCHERA

Ceduna to:

Wirrulla	92km m/h
Poochera	140km c, m/h

Heading east from Ceduna to Port Augusta the highway traverses the Eyre Peninsula, an important wheat growing area. The stretch between Ceduna and Poochera is flat to gently rolling, and crosses open wheat country where winds can be strong. Wirrulla, like all the towns between Ceduna and Kimba, is signalled from a distance by giant grain silos. The town is on a loop road off the main highway and has a shop and a pub.

Somewhere on the road between Wirrulla and Poochera is an important spot on this tour - half way across Australia (Kimba, to the east, uses a different calculation and likes to claim itself as the halfway point).

A sign at the edge of town identifies Poochera as "The Town With A Secret", but does not elaborate. The barmaid at the Poochera pub has the keys to the campground that is next door to the pub. From the campground it's worth taking a walk over the rail line, past the grain silos, and across the highway to the service station. Carefully tended in planters by the pumps here is the SA state symbol - the Desert Sturt Pea - a long blood red blossom with a glossy black spot in the middle.

Poochera is a tiny farming town (population listed as "nominal") sitting between Streaky Bay on the shores of the Great Australian Bight to the west and the Gawler Ranges away to the north-east at the top of the Eyre Peninsula. The Gawler Ranges are a modest line of granite peaks named after George Gawler, the second Governor of SA from 1838 to 1841. Gawler arrived in SA to find the recently established colony in bad shape. Agricultural development was lagging, less than 200 hectares were under cultivation, and almost everything was being imported. He instigated projects to develop SA's own industries and pushed for the rapid development of farmed areas. Gawler is credited with saving the colony from stalling in its early days but his plans suffered from a lack of funds. He spent his budget of £290,000 from the South Australian Company pretty quickly, and started investing his own money. By 1840, the colonist's confidence in SA was restored, but the colony's balance sheet was not looking good, with only £75,000 in revenues, compared to £350,000 in expenditures. Gawler's bills back to London started being refused, and in 1841, he was recalled and George Grey was dispatched to sort out the mess.

Poochera Granite

The granite exposed in the low weatherworn hills around Poochera is the same type of rock that extends 40km below Australia and forms the continental crust on which all other Australian rocks have been deposited.

Granites are formed when molten magma squeezes upward into existing rock and sits slowly cooling in an insulated environment. This slow cooling allows the characteristically large crystals of this rock type time to grow. The mineral crystals in the Poochera granites are easy to see - large clear quartz crystals, pink and white potassium feldspars with distinctive cracks along their cleavage planes, and the platy mica crystals biotite (black) and muscovite (white).

The Poochera granites are thought to be about 600 million years old, old even in geologic terms, but nothing compared to those of the Yilgarn Shield of WA, which are estimated to have formed several billion years earlier. Geologists believe granites that old were the first pieces of continent to rise above the primordial seas. One theory is that magma, sitting intruded in the oceanic crust, cooled so slowly that it allowed the heavier elements to sink and the lighter elements (like those found in granites) to rise - where they eventually bobbed to the surface of the oceanic crust and coalesced into land masses.

A proto-Australia formed in this way would have resulted in a slab of granite tens of kilometres thick, although this basement was far from a stable. The theory of plate tectonics has these early continents jockeying for position and wandering the Earth's surface as if on giant conveyor belts. During various stages in a tumultuous life, Australia has had India wedged along its western coastline, and Antarctica torn off its southern margin. Each collision and tearing apart left a geologic imprint on the continent, and allowed plants and animals to hop on and off. Volcanoes erupted, ice and seas advanced and retreated, and weathering and erosion continued as the continent was buffeted around in slow motion - all these processes contributing to Australia's unique landscape.

Even today, Australia is moving northward at about 8mm a year, on a collision course with Indonesia in about 60 million years.

Camping:
Poochera Hotel, Barnes St, Poochera, Ph (08) 8626 3025, T$8

S$25, D$40 ☐ Poochera Hotel, Barnes St, Poochera, Ph (08) 8626 3025, S$20, D$32

Motel/Hotel:
Wirrulla Hotel, Hay Tce, Wirrulla, Ph (08) 8626 8019,

2000km 8km past Ceduna

2100km 10km past Wirulla

16 POOCHERA TO KIMBA

Poochera to:

Minnipa	33km	c, m/h
Wudinna	72km	c, m/h
Kyancutta	85km	
Kimba	171km	c, m/h, i

Between Poochera and Kimba the road gently rolls through fertile wheat country. Rippling fields cover the rounded granite hills like a patchwork rug over a sleeping giant. Isolated rock formations poke through, with wonderful Aboriginal names of seemingly random letters: Tcharkuldu, Yarwondutta, and Drekurmi. The road smoothly rises and falls over the subdued topography to the small settlement of Minnipa, which includes a service station and store. Wudinna, 39km further on, is a slightly larger town with a bakery and a supermarket.

At the Kyancutta service station, 13km from Wudinna, the road forks, heading south to Port Lincoln at the tip of the Eyre Peninsula, and eastward to Kimba and Port Augusta. Past Kyancutta, the gradual rises and falls of the road become more drawn out and the wheat fields stretch for miles into the distance. On a patch of granite at the crest of one of these rises, is a plaque marking the site where John Drake, an early explorer-surveyor and one of the first Europeans to visit the area, was killed by Aborigines in 1844. He is buried at Drake Peak a hill visible to the south.

Kimba is a supply centre for the surrounding agricultural community and the remote Outback stations to the north. The requirements of the local folk are apparent in the businesses lining the main street - agricultural machinery agents, 4x4 and farm vehicle sales, and a road maintenance depot. On the eastern edge of town are the ubiquitous grain silos, along with and a giant pink parrot perched next to a sign proclaiming the town as "Half-Way Across Australia".

Kimba's Wheat

Kimba is a quintessential wheat belt town, sitting in the shadows of its giant grain storage silos.

Wheat has been grown in Australia since the first fleet sailed into Port Jackson in 1788. Captain Phillip established a convict run farm at Farm Cove and planted 2.5 hectares of English wheat for seed (the site is now the Royal Botanic Gardens in the heart of downtown Sydney). The crop, however, was a disappointment due to the poor soil and harsh climate, and the early Sydney-siders feared they would never be self-sufficient in arable crops. These days wheat is Australia's largest crop in tons produced, area farmed, and export dollars earned.

The turnaround from those early days came after the development of better seed varieties, pest controls, and crop rotation techniques (such as the use of clover ley to improve nitrogen fixation in soils). In 1870, William Farrer, a Cambridge trained mathematician and medical student, immigrated to Australia in the hope of curing his tuberculosis. He took up farming near Queanbeyan (now on the outskirts of Canberra) and used his background in maths and medicine to selectively crossbreed a drought and rust resistant wheat variety known as "Federation Wheat". This new variety was much better suited to Australian conditions and was used across the country for decades (Farrer's portrait appeared on the Australian $2 note until it was replaced by a coin). The application of superphosphate fertilisers, starting in the early 1900's, has also greatly assisted production.

1919 Daisy Bates (once married to folk hero Breaker Morant) arrives at Ooldea, north of Nundroo, where she provides food and medical help to Aborigines for the next 14 years

Australia has grown into the worlds fourth largest exporter of wheat, and the crop is grown in every state. The annual production almost always exceeds 500 million bushels, which is worth about $A2 billion to the economy.

Most of this wheat is grown in the "Wheat Belt", a climatically favourable strip running across the country - with a noticeable gap across the Nullarbor - where wheat growing becomes a generally profitable enterprise. Interestingly, sole proprietors or family businesses run the vast majority (90%) of Australia's wheat farms, with the average farm being quite small - about 1,000 hectares. All the nations production destined for export is marketed through the Australian Wheat Board, and the principal destination is Asia (primarily China, Japan, Indonesia and Korea). In good years over a million tonnes are shipped to each of these countries - a volume which the first Sydney farmers would have had difficulty comprehending.

Camping:
Minnipa Caravan Park, Eyre Hwy, Minnipa, Ph (08) 8680 5175, T$5 ☐ Gawler Ranges Motel & Caravan Park, Eyre Hwy, Wudinna, Ph (08) 8680 2090, T$9 ☐ Kimba Motel Roadhouse & Caravan Park, Eyre Hwy, Kimba, Ph (08) 8627 2040, T$10

Motel/Hotel:
Minnipa Hotel-Motel, Railway Tce, Minnipa, Ph (08) 8680 5005, S$50, D$60 ☐ Gawler Ranges Motel, Eyre Hwy, Wudinna, Ph (08) 8680 2090, S$68, D$77

☐ Wudinna Hotel-Motel, Burton Tce, Wudinna, Ph (08) 8680 2019, S$58, D$68 ☐ Kimba Community Hotel-Motel, High St, Kimba, Ph (08) 8627 2007, S$30, D$50 ☐ Kimba Motel Roadhouse, Eyre Hwy, Kimba, Ph (08) 8627 2040, S$55, D$65

i:
The Big Galah, Eyre Hwy, Kimba, Ph (08) 8627 2112

2200km 5km before Wudinna

2300km 8km before Kimba

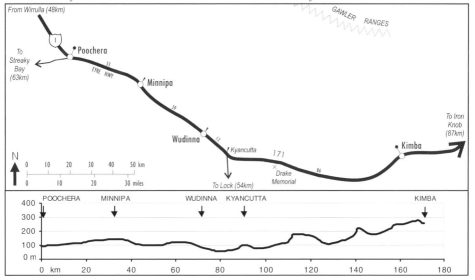

17 KIMBA TO PORT AUGUSTA

Kimba to:

Iron Knob   87km   m/h, i
Port Augusta   155km c, m/h, i, bike shop

This stage leaves the wheat growing area of the Eyre Peninsula behind and passes through the Lake Gillies Conservation Park before reaching the mining town of Iron Knob. From here it's another 68km to Port Augusta - the first real city since Perth.

The road is gently rolling out of Kimba until Lake Gillies Park, where it becomes rolling to hilly. On the other side of the park it reverts back to gently rolling terrain and then, 20km before Iron Knob, the road flattens and gradually drops to Port Augusta.

Rather than becoming increasingly inhabited towards the city of Port Augusta, the countryside past Kimba returns to scrappy bush, and there is almost no sign of civilisation until Iron Knob. The road through the Lake Gillies Conservation Park traverses a sandy scrub wilderness that seems to have little economic value (probably why it has been designated a nature reserve). For miles ahead the road can be seen climbing and dropping over the large sandy ridges - the first decent hills since WA.

Scraggly farmland reappears on the other side of park but dies out again before Iron Knob as the road crosses a barren plain with the flattened hilltop of "The Knob" in the distance. This mine, along with others in area like Iron Baron, Iron Monarch, Iron Duke, and Iron Duchess, has supplied iron ore to Port Pirie's blast furnaces for over 100 years. An impressive collection of rocks and crystals from these mines are on display in the local museum and in Adelaide's museum. Iron Knob itself is 1km south of the highway, past an enormous (now retired) electric shovel. Production at the mine has been scaled back in recent years due to the development of large iron ore reserves in WA, and the town is in decline - a sorry collection of miners shacks and unkempt buildings.

Past Iron Knob the highway is smooth and wide, dropping gently across a plain to the low ranges on the skyline. The road finds a way between the hills and on the other side joins the Lincoln Highway from Whyalla. The last 26km into Port Augusta are busy with a constant stream of cars and trucks. On the outskirts of Port Augusta, there is an ignominious end to one of Australia's great road journeys - a spray-painted sign on a lamppost marking the end of the Eyre Highway.

Port Augusta is a bustling little city - a crossroads for travellers heading north to Darwin, west to Perth, and south to Adelaide. It's also a jumping off point for a smaller number of people heading into the Outback. The smooth watered lawns and swimming pools of Port Augusta's campgrounds are a refreshing change from the dusty camping patches of the Nullarbor.

Iron Knobs Iron Mine

Since 1880, generations of men have won iron ore from the low hills surrounding Iron Knob - the birthplace of Australia's steel industry. The explorer Edward Eyre passed through this area in 1839 and, climbing to the top of one of the hills, recognised ironstone underfoot. Today, Iron Knob is conspicuously flat topped, 150m lower than when Eyre passed by, and getting lower as mining continues. The company that runs the mine, BHP, basically established the town.

BHP (The Broken Hill Proprietary Company) is Australia's largest company; an industrial giant built on mining and steel production. The company started after Charles Rasp's 1884 discovery of the world's biggest silver-zinc-lead lode, at Broken Hill in NSW. BHP boomed and in 1899 the company took up the Iron Knob lease to supply ironstone flux to its smelters at Port Pirie, which processed the Broken Hill ore. By

1922 The first lock on the Murray River is built at Blanchetown

1915, BHP was also loading Iron Knob ore onto ships at Whyalla for transport to its new steel mill at Newcastle, NSW. During World War II, iron from the Knob supported Whyalla's ship building industry and a blast furnace made artillery shells.

In 1958, BHP, encouraged by the SA Government, which was keen to process the ore in-state, started construction of a complete steel milling operation at Whyalla, and the town has grown into the second largest city in SA. As the principal supplier to BHP's steelworks for over 70 years, the Iron Knob mines helped build the company to its present colossal size, but the discovery of iron deposits in northern WA has reduced the Knob's significance and BHP has scaled back its operations here to under 100 men. Riding down the main street it's clear from the empty shops and houses that the town is shrinking. On the way into Iron Knob a gigantic electric digger (the "shovellaurus"), which worked the mine for decades, sits as a legacy to the town's past.

Camping:
Big 4 Holiday Park, Cnr Highway 1 & Stokes Tce, Port Augusta, Ph (08) 8642 2974, T$10 ☐ Shoreline Caravan Park, Gardiner Ave, Port Augusta West, Ph (08) 8642 2965, T$10 ☐ Others; Port Augusta

Motel/Hotel:
Iron Knob Motel Roadhouse, Eyre Highway, Iron Knob, Ph (08) 8646 2058, S$40, D$50 ☐ Flinders Hotel-Motel, 39 Commercial Rd, Port Augusta, Ph (08) 8642 2544, S$38, D$47 ☐ Myoora Motor Inn, 10 Eyre Hwy, Port Augusta, Ph (08) 8642 3622, S$57,

D$67 ☐ Augusta Westside Motel, 3 Loudon Rd, Port Augusta, Ph (08) 8642 2488, S$58, D$62 ☐ Others; Iron Knob, Port Augusta

i:
Iron Knob Tourist Centre & Mine Tours, Iron Knob, Ph (08) 8646 2129 ☐ Pt Augusta Information Centre, 41 Flinders Tce, Port Augusta, Ph (08) 8641 0793

Bike Shops:
Cycle Worx, Port Augusta, 4 Church St, Port Augusta, Ph (08) 8642 4577 ☐ Flinders Cycles, 1 Hospital Rd, Port Augusta, Ph (08) 8641 0269

2400km 1km before Iron Knob

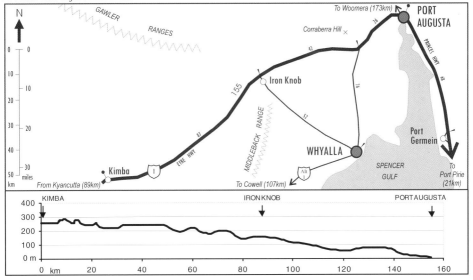

ALTERNATIVE: ACROSS THE RED CENTRE

Note: This route crosses some of the remotest and hottest parts of Australia and should only be considered by bike after some serious research.

Leaving Port Augusta the Stuart Highway heads north 173km without a break to Pimba and the rocket and weapon-testing town of Woomera (7km off the highway). Britain undertook experimental nuclear explosions near here in the 1950's. In the Outback beyond Woomera is the gold and uranium-mining town of Roxby Downs. Glendambo is the last stop before the 253km uninhabited stretch to Coober Pedy, an opal-mining town. Most accommodation at Coober Pedy is underground to avoid the heat and the town's name is Aboriginal for "White mans hole in the ground". There are only a couple of tiny stops between here and Kulgera in southern NT.

74km north of Kulgera is Erldunda and the turn off to Uluru (Ayers Rock), Australia's most famous piece of geology, 244km to the west. 69km north of Erldunda is Henbury, which has a series of meteorite craters nearby.

Alice Springs is the largest stop between Port Augusta and Darwin and is a big tourist town. Located in the MacDonnell Ranges, "Alice" started out as a telegraph repeater station supplied by camel trains from Port Augusta. Today, the town is a gateway for travellers to Ayers Rock, The Olgas, and Kings Canyon. Aileron and Barrow Creek are both small Outback settlements. Just beyond Warchope is the Devils Marbles Conservation Reserve where erosion has left huge granite boulders balancing precariously. Tennant Creek is a mining town located, reputedly, at the spot where a wagon hauling beer broke down and the driver gave up and drank the cargo. After Tennant Creek the highway passes memorials to John Flynn - a Presbyterian minister who initiated the Royal Flying Doctor Service, and John Stuart - who passed this way in 1862 en route to Australia's northern coast. Stuart, who had been on Charles Sturt's 1844 expedition to Central Australia, reached the north coast on his third attempt and was awarded a £2,000 prize and 1,000 acres of land rent-free for 7 years.

As the highway heads north it passes through a succession of small stops with diminutive populations. At Mataranka there is a tourist resort with hot mineral pools surrounded by tropical forest, and you can take a 4-wheel drive tour or try barramundi fishing. Katherine is a bigger tourist destination with the spectacular Katherine Gorge National Park nearby. Boat trips inside the gorge are a popular activity. Pine Creek and Adelaide River are small settlements before Darwin with mining histories.

Darwin is Australia's northern most city and is famous for being bombed by the Japanese on 19 February 1942 (243 people killed), and the devastating 1974 "Cyclone Tracy", which hit on Christmas Day and pretty much levelled the town (50 people killed). Today tourism is a major industry. With Asia just across the water; army, navy, and airforce bases are located nearby. Possible stages in a south-north crossing could be:

Port Augusta to Woomera (180km) ⬡ Woomera to Glendambo (120km) ⬡ Glendambo to Free camp (126km) ⬡ Free camp to Coober Pedy (127km) ⬡ Coober Pedy to Cadney Park Roadhouse (150km) ⬡ Cadney Park Roadhouse to Marla (83km) ⬡ Marla to Kulgera (178km) ⬡ Kulgera to Erldunda (74km) ⬡ Erldunda to Henbury (68km) ⬡ Henbury to Alice Springs (130km) ⬡ Alice Springs to Aileron (133km) ⬡ Aileron to Barrow Creek (149km) ⬡ Barrow Creek to Warchope (110km) ⬡ Warchope to Tennant Creek (115km) ⬡ Tennant Creek to Renner Spring (160km) ⬡ Renner Spring to Elliot (92km) ⬡ Elliot to Daly Waters (145km) ⬡ Daly Waters to Mataranka (164km) ⬡ Mataranka to Katherine (106km) ⬡ Katherine to Pine Creek (89km) ⬡ Pine Creek to Adelaide River (113km) ⬡ Adelaide River to Darwin (113km)

1929 A train runs from Adelaide to Alice Springs for the first time

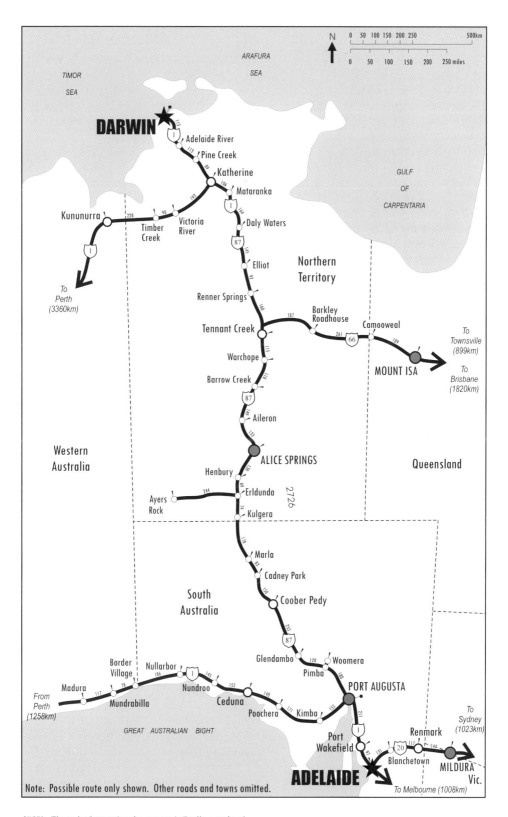

1930's The task of surveying the country is finally completed

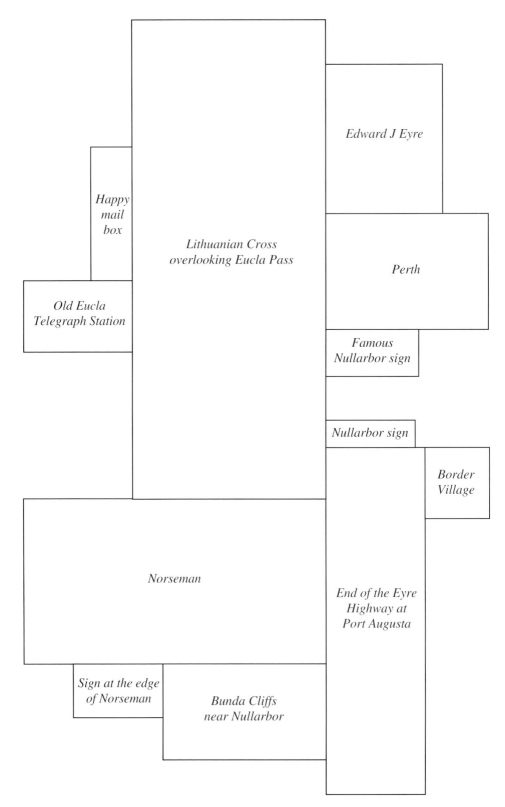

Edward J Eyre

Happy
mail
box

Lithuanian Cross
overlooking Eucla Pass

Perth

Old Eucla
Telegraph Station

Famous
Nullarbor sign

Nullarbor sign

Border
Village

Norseman

End of the Eyre
Highway at
Port Augusta

Sign at the edge
of Norseman

Bunda Cliffs
near Nullarbor

*1930 Rolf Harris, composer of "Tie Me Kangaroo Down
Sport", is born*

*1930 The depression hits and a new wave of swagmen walk the
Outback looking for work*

KEY:

0km	100km	200km
300km	400km	500km
600km	700km	800km
900km	1000km	1100km
1200km	1300km	1400km
1500km	1600km	1700km
1800km	1900km	2000km
2100km	2200km	

*1930   The Aboriginal population declines to 70,000, its lowest
point since European settlement*

2300km	2400km	2500km
2600km	2700km	2800km
2900km	3000km	3100km
3200km	3300km	3400km
3500km	3600km	3700km
3800km	3900km	4000km
4100km	4200km	4300km
4302km		

KEY:

1932 At the Sydney Harbour Bridge opening Francis De Groot gallops
up, slashes the ribbon with his sword, announces "On behalf of the
decent citizens of NSW, I declare this bridge open", and is arrested

1934 An airmail service between England and Australia starts

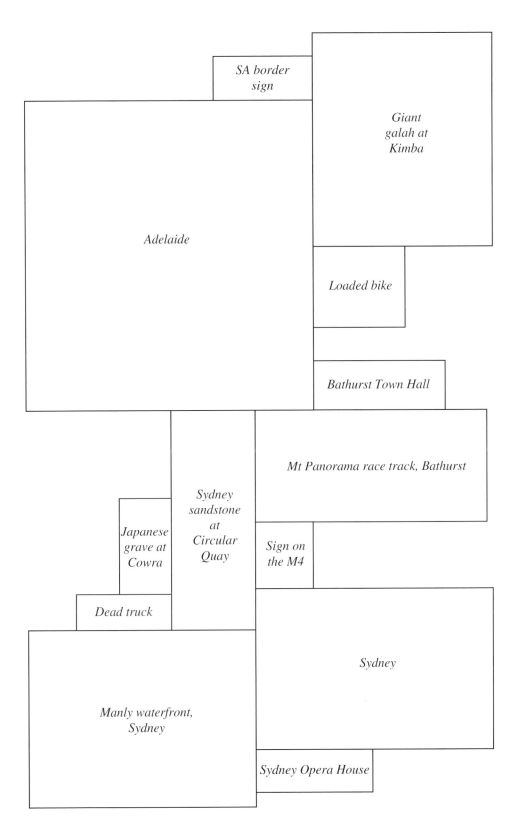

SA border
sign

Giant
galah at
Kimba

Adelaide

Loaded bike

Bathurst Town Hall

Mt Panorama race track, Bathurst

Sydney
sandstone
at
Circular
Quay

Japanese
grave at
Cowra

Sign on
the M4

Dead truck

Sydney

Manly waterfront,
Sydney

Sydney Opera House

1935 "The Cattle King" Sidney Kidman dies. After starting out with a one-eyed horse and 5 shillings, he dies owning over 100 stations and a huge chunk of Australia

Port Augusta to:

Port Pirie	89km c, m/h, bike shop
Crystal Brook	110km c, m/h
Snowtown	162km m/h
Port Wakefield	211km c, m/h

Port Augusta to Port Wakefield is a big haul - a journey that could easily be split into two, with a stay at either Port Pirie (89km) or Crystal Brook (110km). The route is flat or gently rolling apart from two stretches of climbs, one before Crystal Brooke and one after Lochiel.

On the outskirts of Port Augusta, the road passes coal-fired power stations that generate a third of SA's electricity - the black smoke from the stacks will indicate whether the wind direction is favourable for cycling. The road runs south across a farmed plain between the Flinders Ranges on the left and the Spencer Gulf on the right.

Port Germain and Port Pirie are both short side trips off the main highway. Port Germain is a small beach resort while Port Pirie, marked by tall chimneys, is an industrial town that processes silver-zinc-lead ore from the Broken Hill mine in NSW. The town's lead-smelters are the largest in the world and BHP, the company that owns the smelter, runs tours of the operation. After the Port Pirie turnoff, the road turns inland across wheat growing country crowning the top of the Yorke Peninsula. Port Victoria on the west coast of this peninsula was once a bustling port where sailing ships loaded grain before racing each other to Europe. The last one sailed in 1949.

Crystal Brooke has a campground and a reptile farm where you can watch venomous snakes being milked (the venom is used in making snakebite serum). The bridge at Crystal Brooke crosses the rail line bringing the Broken Hill ore to Port Pirie in open cars.

Snowtown, 162km from Port Augusta, is a pretty little rural town. Don't plan on arriving on a Saturday afternoon when the local Aussie Rules Football team is playing though, the main street will probably be deserted and you are likely to find a note on a door reading "Good Luck Crows - Back At 4:00pm". 18km after Snowtown and 31km before Port Wakefield is Lochiel (a pub and a saltworks on the edge of Lake Bumbunga).

On the fringes of Port Wakefield are a strip of service stations and fast food outlets, but past these the town is charming, with wide old streets, solid stone buildings, and graceful wooden homes with tall palms. A monument to Matthew Flinders, who sailed past here and named the spot, sits on the foreshore.

The Stump Jumper and the Grain Race

A revolution took place in Australian farming after the Stump Jump plough was invented near Port Wakefield in 1876. With this new plough farmers avoided having to dig out the tree roots in recently broken-in land before they could cultivate. As a result, large areas in SA and Vic., previously covered in stunted mallee, were quickly turned into productive farmland covered with sheep and wheat farms.

Two brothers, Richard and Clarence Smith, are credited with the idea for the Stump Jumper, although a bitter feud ensued between the brothers over who actually developed the plough. Richard was 18 years older than Clarence and had a successful coach building business in Port Wakefield when his father asked him to apprentice young Clarrie. According to local lore Richard was ploughing a field one day when a bolt holding the plough's fluke broke. Rather than fixing it he carried on, finding it actually worked better than before by lifting itself over buried stumps with ease. The two brothers worked on a prototype that was exhibited at the 1876 Regional Agricultural Show. Richard won first prize - but the plans were signed by Clarence. After his apprenticeship Clarence started his own company and both men continued making and developing their own Stump Jumper designs. In 1882, the SA government paid Richard a £500 reward for the invention, but in some circles there was suspicion that Clarrie was the brains behind the design. Bad blood between the brothers followed and although they never reconciled, history now credits both of them with the invention.

The new plough meant a jump in wheat production for the burgeoning grain trade between Australia and Europe. Known as "The Grain Race" this involved tall ships sailing around the bottom of Africa and eastward across the Indian Ocean to load Australian wheat at Port Victoria or Port Lincoln. The ships, known as Windjammers, then raced each other eastwards around Cape Horn to Europe. The fastest return voyage was in 1933 - the England to England trip taking just 83 days.

Camping:
Port Germein Caravan Park, c/- the Post Office, Port Germein, Ph (08) 8634 5266, T$10 ☐ Port Pirie Beach Caravan Park, Beach Rd, Port Pirie, Ph (08) 8632 4275, T$10 ☐ Crystal Brook Caravan Park, Eyre Rd, Crystal Brook, Ph (08) 8636 2640, T$8 ☐ Port Wakefield Caravan Park, Wakefield St, Port Wakefield SA 5550, Ph (08) 8867 1151, T$8 ☐ Others; Port Pirie,

Motel/Hotel:
International Hotel-Motel, 40 Ellen St, Port Pirie, Ph (08) 8632 2422, S$20, D$32 ☐ Flinders Range Motor Inn, 151 Main Rd, Port Pirie, Ph (08) 8632 3555, S$70, D$75 ☐ Crystal Brook Hotel, 47 Railway Tce, Crystal Brook, Ph (08) 8636 2023, S$18, D$30 ☐ Snowtown Hotel, 52 Railway Tce, Snowtown, Ph (08) 8865 2256, S$20, D$40 ☐ Port Wakefield Hotel, Main Rd, Port Wakefield, Ph (08) 8867 1271, S$35, D$45 ☐ Others; Port Pirie, Crystal Brooke,

Bike Shop:
Cycle Works, 99 Florence St, Port Pirie, Ph (08) 8632 1219

2500km 30km past Port Augusta

2600km 30km before Snowtown

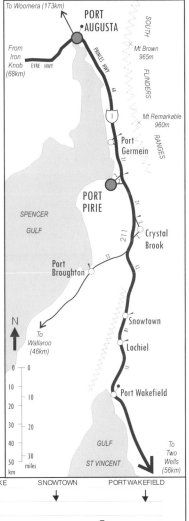

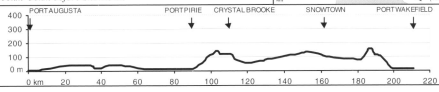

Port Wakefield to:

Two Wells	56km	c, m/h
Adelaide	97km	c, h, m/h, i, bike shop

This is a flat stage and with a strong tail wind you'll be racing tumbleweeds to Two Wells. Unfortunately the road gets busier all the way to Adelaide. En route the wide-open farmland progressively changes to the smaller parcels of land which city-folk like to own and the highway becomes double laned for the first time since Perth - split down the middle by a ragged grass verge. Watch for the cats-eyes reflectors on the roadside along this stretch, these give an unnerving jolt to the front wheel when ridden over.

The highway passes pint-sized stops like Wild Horse Plains, Windsor, and Dublin before reaching the small town of Two Wells, 41km before Adelaide (there were a couple of Aboriginal wells near here when Europeans settled the area - hence the name). Accommodation and services are available just off the highway.

Past Two Wells the traffic increases significantly and takes on a generally frenetic air. The fields give way to market gardens, and the market gardens finally fade into car sales yards, furniture discounters, and mall parking lots. The road passes through the suburbs of Enfield, Blair Athol, and Prospect before reaching North Adelaide's tree lined streets. The city's best features are the 700-hectare green belt, which surrounds the central business district, and the Torrens River, which runs through the middle of the city separating Adelaide and North Adelaide.

Adelaide is the fourth largest city in Australia and likes to market itself as the festival city. The biggest of these is the Adelaide Festival of Arts, which has been held here in March of every even numbered year since 1960. The festival draws an international crowd and is Australia's showcase for home-grown musicians, artists, dancers and film-makers. During the festival is a great time to visit Adelaide as the city is pretty much one big party for three weeks (book ahead for accommodation if you're planning to pass through town around this time).

The city lost a major draw card a few years back. During the festival the city centre used to host a street race on the World Formula 1 Grand Prix circuit. That was until Melbourne stole it away from SA in a controversial coup.

The Don and the Bodyline Test

The leafy Adelaide cricket oval, with its wooden benches and white picket fence, was the site in January 1933 of Australia's most infamous sporting incident. During the English cricket tour that year England's bowlers, in an attempt to counter the phenomenal run scoring of Australia's Donald Bradman, deployed a controversial "Body-line" technique. They consistently bowled fast bouncing deliveries aimed at the batsmen's body and head, forcing the batter to play into an area of the field loaded with opposing players. Tensions climaxed during the final test in Adelaide when Australia's wicket-keeper, Bert Oldfield, was struck on the head by an English delivery. The Australian captain, hit twice by bouncers himself, accused England in a now immortalised comment of "not playing cricket".

There was serious talk at the time of cancelling the tour, but England went on to win the test, and the series (although what many Adelaide folk remember is that the night watchman, Walter Mummery, had to guard the pitch against sabotage with a 12-gauge shotgun).

Born in Cootamundara, NSW in 1908 Sir Donald Bradman ("The Don") still lives in

Adelaide, the site of that famous 1933 test match. In cricket circles he is undisputedly regarded as the greatest test batter ever. His test career started against England in the 1928-29 series, and ending famously against England at Lords, London in 1948, when he was bowled for a duck (no score) needing only four runs to carry his career average to 100. His average of 99.94 is still considered incredible (the nearest anyone else has come, before or since, is an average of just over 60).

The BBC recently paid tribute to Bradman, including interviews with some of the players who came up against him. Godfrey Evans played against Bradman in that final series in England; "Out there in the middle, when he'd been there a while, I'd say to him "How's your wife?" and he'd say "I'll tell you after I've finished batting." You couldn't get the concentration out of him. His greatest strength was that every time he went to the wicket, he would score 100. You don't want much more strength than that. Don't forget he scored 300 in a day off Harold Larwood *(England's best bowler at the time)*. Not a bad effort". Richie Benaud, an ex-Australian captain, was even more effusive; "He is the greatest Australian that ever lived."

Cricket is still Australia's passion during summer, and Bradman truly is a national icon. On The Don's 90th birthday, the Australian Prime Minister John Howard's comments were; "the greatest living Australian, more than just a supreme cricketer, a beacon of hope for a generation living through the dark economic days of the Great Depression, and inspiration to a generation of Australians when the memories of the terrible slaughter of our young men in France and on the beaches of Gallipoli was still very much part of the Australian psyche."

(Note: For Adelaide details see p.86)
Camping:
Middle Beach Caravan Park, 5 Recreation Dr, <u>Two</u> <u>Wells</u>, Ph (08) 8520 2374, T$10

Motel/Hotel:
Two Wells Motel, Main St, <u>Two</u> <u>Wells</u>, Ph (08) 8520 2052, S$45, D$55

2700km 16km past Port Wakefield

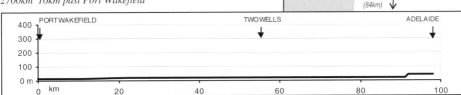

1943 A floating bridge is opened across Hobart's Derwent River. At 965m it becomes the longest in the world

85

ADELAIDE

Adelaide is an ordered and leafy contrast to the predominantly arid countryside covering much of SA. The city centre is divided in two by the gentle **Torrens River**. Public **parks** and **gardens** line the riverbanks, which at lunchtime are dotted with sandwich eating office workers - lounging with their shoes off and sleeves rolled up. A ring of parks, sports fields and playgrounds surrounds the city, completely encircling the downtown area and separating it from the suburbs. The city's location and thoughtful layout are the work of Lieutenant-Colonel William Light, who in 1836 stepped ashore to become SA's first Surveyor-General.

The grid of north-south and east-west trending streets makes it easy to navigate around Adelaide. King William St, which becomes King William Rd, is the main thoroughfare and **Victoria Square** is essentially the middle of the city with the **Central Market**, **Post Office** and **civic buildings** nearby.

Many of Adelaides attractions are on, or near, North Tce, which runs parallel to the Torrens River. A walk along North Tce from west to east passes **Old Parliament House**, a newer **Parliament House** (where the state legislature meets), and across the road behind a stone wall, **Government House** (the oldest building in the city and the State Premier's residence). The **SA Museum** has good displays of Aboriginal and Pacific culture, Australian minerals and wildlife, and in their bookstore; a live Death Adder. Next door to the museum is the **Art Gallery of SA** with an excellent collection of native and settler art. The gallery has works by Tom Roberts whose bush paintings, such as *A Break Away!* (1891) and *Shearing the Rams* (1890), are Aussie classics.

The **Migration Museum** on Kintore Avenue is one of the most interesting museums in Adelaide. Housed in the city's former Destitute Asylum, it tells the stories of the families who immigrated to SA in the 19th and 20th Centuries. Cultural Adelaide, is centred around the **Adelaide Festival Centre**, which has an eclectic mix of entertainment and hosts Australia's biggest arts festival in March of even-numbered years.

North of the river is the **Adelaide Oval**, where international cricket tests are played and the infamous 1933 body-line test took place. Just north of the Oval is **St Peter's Cathedral**, designed by William Butterfield in gothic revival style.

Short trips outside Adelaide include the nearby **valleys** and **vineyards** of the **Adelaide Hills**, and **Mount Lofty** with good views over the city. **Port Adelaide** has a marine museum, and a rail museum with a "Tea and Sugar" train that used to supply the Nullarbor settlements. The nearby **city beaches** are pretty - at **Glenelg** is the **Gum Tree** under which Lieutenant-Colonel Light proclaimed the Colony of SA on his arrival.

Camping:
Adelaide Caravan Park, Bruton St, Hackney, Ph (08) 8363 1566, T$23 (3km NE of downtown, gravel sites only) ☐ West Beach Caravan Park, 1 Military Rd, West Beach, Ph (08) 8356 7654, T$18 (9km W of downtown) ☐ Adelaide Beachfront Tourist Park, 349 Military Rd, Semaphore Park, Ph (08) 8449 7726, T$19 (14km NW of downtown) ☐ Others; Adelaide

Hostel:
Adelaide Backpackers Inn, 112 Carrington St, Adelaide, Ph (08) 8223 6635, Dm$18, S$33, D$48 ☐ Adelaide City YHA, 290 Gilles Street, Adelaide, Ph (08) 8223 6007, Dm$16, D$46 ☐ East Park Lodge, 341 Agnas St, Adelaide, Ph (08) 8223 1228, Dm$19, S$39, D$49 ☐ Others; Adelaide

Motel/Hotel:
Adelaide City Parklands Motel, 471 Pulteney St, Adelaide, Ph (08) 8223 1444, S$65, D$76 ☐ Adelaide Paringa Motel, 15 Hindley St, Adelaide, Ph (08) 8231 1000, S$88, D$107 ☐ Adelaide Riviera Motel, 31 North Tce, Adelaide, Ph (08) 8231 8000, S$105, D$105 ☐ Others; Adelaide

i:
SA Travel Centre, 1 King William St, Adelaide, Ph (08) 212 1505 or 1 800 882 092

Bike Shops:
Super Elliotts, 200 Rundle St, Adelaide, Ph (08) 8223 3946 ☐ J.T. Cycles, 234 Pulteney St, Adelaide, Ph (08) 8359 2755 ☐ Others; Adelaide

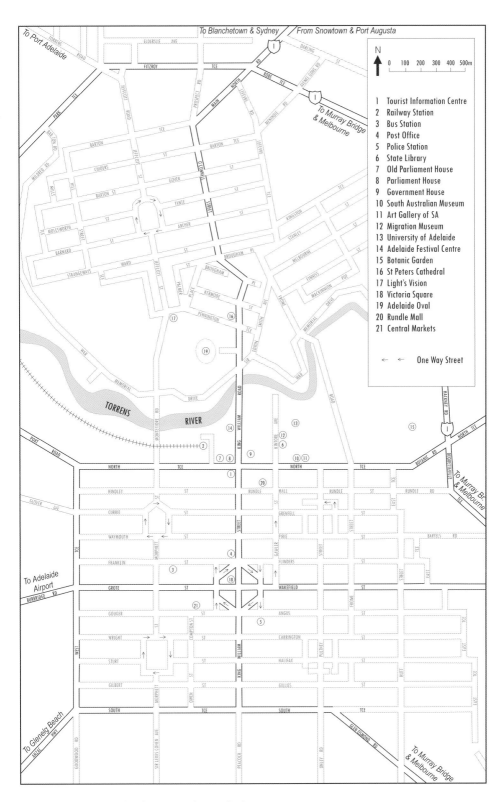

ALTERNATIVE: SYDNEY VIA MELBOURNE

The Princes Highway to Melbourne touches a beautiful and varied coastline in places. Soon after leaving Adelaide the road passes the mouth of the Murray River at Lake Alexandrina, named in 1830 after Princess Alexandrina (later Queen Victoria). From here the road parallels the inland side of the Younghusband Peninsula, beside the slender body of saltwater known as "The Coorong". This National Park is famous for its wildlife, especially its birds, which include black swans, ibis, and pelicans.

At Kingston SE the highway heads inland to Mt Gambier, a large town situated on the edge of an extinct volcano. One of the four crater lakes here inexplicably turns bright blue every year in November, then reverts back to grey after three months. The exotic pine plantations in this area are the largest in Australia.

Across the border in Vic. the road touches the coast again at Portland, Port Fairy, and Peterborough. Peterborough (about 55km after Warrnambool) is the start of The Great Ocean Road on Hwy 100, a 300km stretch that includes spectacular coastal cliffs, the "12 Apostles" sea stacks, and some of the country's best surf spots. Geelong is a commercial and industrial centre just before Australia's second largest city, Melbourne.

Melbourne - the sensible sister to Sydney - has retained its old electric trams, Victorian buildings and public parks. It also has a reputation for great food and fanatical sports fans, particularly for Australian Rules Football, a game invented here.

East of Melbourne the Princes Highway passes through dairy farmland before the coal mining and power generating area of Morwell in the Latrobe Valley. Between Sale

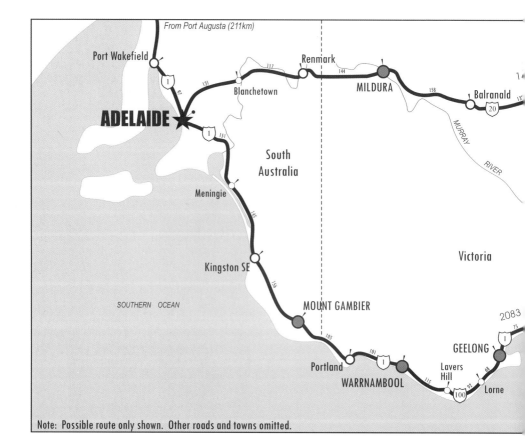

Note: Possible route only shown. Other roads and towns omitted.

1948 Don Bradman plays cricket for Australia for the last time. Needing 4 runs to take his test average over 100, he is bowled for a duck (no score)

(63km after Morwell) and Lakes Entrance (36km after Bairnsdale) the highway passes to the north of the Gippsland Lakes Coastal Park and The Lakes National Park, two areas of outstanding beauty.

After Lakes Entrance the road passes through a number of small farming and timber towns, including Orbost on the Snowy River - a river made famous in Banjo Paterson's "The Man From Snowy River". The road briefly passes through three small National Parks then turns northward before the first sizeable town in NSW - Eden (54km past Genoa). From here the highway heads up the eastern seaboard alternating between seaside towns on the Pacific and inland farming areas. Heading north, the towns become progressively more populated and the route follows a coastline first mapped by Cook in 1770.

Wollongong, 86km south of Sydney, is a coal and steel town that also caters to tourists. North over the Bulli Pass the road passes through the Royal National Park before reaching Sydney. A possible route for Adelaide to Sydney, via Melbourne is:

Adelaide to Meningie (151km) ❑ Meningie to Kingston SE (145km) ❑ Kingston SE to Mt Gambia (156 km) ❑ Mt Gambier to Portland (105km) ❑ Portland to Warrnambool (101km) ❑ Warrnambool to Lavers Hill (115 km) ❑ Lavers Hill to Lorne (92km) ❑ Lorne to Geelong (68km) ❑ Geelong to Melbourne (75km) ❑ Melbourne to Morwell (150km) ❑ Morwell to Bairnsdale (132km) ❑ Bairnsdale to Orbost (97km) ❑ Orbost to Genoa (125km) ❑ Genoa to Merimbula (90km) ❑ Merimbula to Narooma (113km) ❑ Narooma to Ulladulla (121km) ❑ Ulladulla to Shellharbour (129km) ❑ Shellharbour to Sydney (118km)

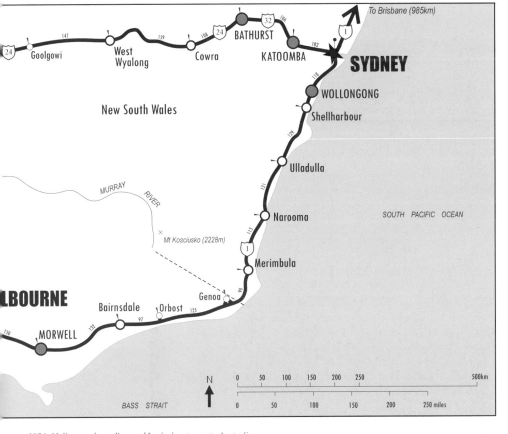

Adelaide to:

Gawler	42km	c, m/h, i, bike shop
Nuriootpa	73km	c, m/h
Blanchetown	131km	c

Leaving Adelaide for the Murray River requires backtracking on your route into the city for 10km, to the Gawler turn-off and the start of the Sturt Highway. The road is busy until Elizabeth (25km), with virtually no shoulder and a constant stream of vehicles at your elbow. Past Elizabeth the traffic thins as the suburbs are left behind. The quickest route to Blanchetown is to stay on the Sturt Highway, bypass central Gawler, and head directly towards Nuriootpa in the north of the Barossa Valley. If you do stop at Gawler check out the town clock tower, which was accidentally constructed with two 9's on the dial.

The route climbs steadily to Truro, a small settlement with a pub and motel, then drops onto the Murray River plain and is practically flat to Blanchetown.

A slightly longer and hillier route to Nuriootpa, but the one you'll want to take if you like good wine, is "The Barossa Way". This alternative passes through the southern and central regions of Australia's most famous wine producing area and has plenty of opportunities for wine tasting. The SA Travel Centre in Adelaide has details on this route.

Nuriootpa is on a short signposted loop off the Sturt Highway and is a good place to stop for lunch. The road into town passes vine-covered fields that produce some of the nation's best wine. Nuriootpa is a busy town with a good selection of shops. The towns discoloured water comes from the Murray River and you'll appreciate the difference if you can get a friendly local to fill up your drink bottles from their rain tank.

After Truro, a small village marked by huge gum trees hanging over the highway, the road passes through some stony paddocks until a huge flat appears below. This is the ancient flood plain of the Murray River, the result of the rivers meanderings.

Blanchetown is perched on the edge of the plain, looking down on the Murray's current course. The road to the campground drops over a lip and descends the old riverbank. The river is wide, brown, and fast flowing here.

Blanchetown was proclaimed a port in 1863 based on the volume of the river traffic that passed, and the town had a service for punting horse-drawn coaches across the river. Crossings by punt continued until 1964 when the road bridge was finally built. Lock 1 is next to the campground. Built in 1922 this was the first of 26 locks constructed along the river. You can walk across the lock during the day and watch pelicans and shags fishing in the disturbed water.

Barossa History

Barossa owes its reputation for fine wine, in part, to the King of Prussia's persecution of Lutherans in the 1830's. Friedrich Wilhelm III's edict to join the state church was rejected by the Lutherains, and they suffered for it. Soldiers drove them from their churches, and non-state marriages and baptisms were declared illegal. Pastors found performing them were imprisoned, and baptised children were automatically re-baptised into the state church.

After 10 years of passive resistance, many of the Lutherans decided to emigrate. Pastor Augustus Kavel was elected their leader and while investigating Russia or America as potential destinations he met George Angas in London. Angas was a capitalist and philanthropist who had recently persuaded the British Government to establish the South Australian Company, with himself as a director. Angas was sympathetic towards the Lutherans and saw the Germans as ideal potential settlers. With

1955 Power is generated from the huge Snowy Mountains Hydroelectric Scheme for the first time

funds provided by Angas, the first Lutherans arrived on 25 November 1838, only 2 years after the SA colony had been established. The names of those early Germans settlers are now synonymous with success in the wine industry; Seppelt, Gramp, Sobels and Penfold.

The Barossa area was first surveyed in 1841, with 28,000 acres in the valley purchased by Angus himself at a cost of £1 an acre. Much of this land was made available to the Lutherans, and in 1842 many families settled near Bethany. Angas himself followed in 1850, the year the first wine was produced.

Today, many businesses are still run by those original wine making families and there are more than 30 Lutheran churches in the area, many built from local limestone.

Camping:
Gawler Caravan Park, Main North Rd, Gawler, Ph (08) 8522 3805, T$11 ☐ Nuriootpa Caravan Tourist Park, Penrice Rd, Nuriootpa, Ph (08) 8562 1404, T$11 ☐ Riverside Caravan Park, Sanders St, Blanchetown, Ph (08) 8540 5070, T$14 ☐ Blanchetown Caravan Park, River Dr, Blanchetown, Ph (08) 8540 5073, T$14☐ ☐ River Palm Caravan Park, River Dr, Blanchetown, Ph (08) 8540 5035, T$14

Motel/Hotel:
Gawler By-Pass Motel, 1 Main North Rd, Gawler, Ph (08) 8522 5900, S$50, D$50 ☐ Barossa Gateway Motel, Kalimna Rd, Nuriootpa, Ph (08) 8562 1033, S$32, D$42 ☐ Top of the Valley Tourist Motel, 49 Murray St, Nuriootpa, Ph (08) 8562 2111, S$55, D$63

☐ Truro Hotel, Moorundie St, Truro, Ph (08) 8564 0218, *(re-opening 2001)* ☐ Barossa Ranges Weightbridge Motel, PO Box 228, Truro, Ph (08) 8564 0400, S$40, D$60 ☐ Also: Check Blanchetown caravan parks for on-site cabins

i:
Gawler Visitor Centre, 2 Lyndoch Rd, Gawler, Ph (08) 8522 6814

Bike Shops:
Trak Cycles, Elizabeth City Centre, Elizabeth, Ph (08) 8255 2400 ☐ Elizabeth Star Cycles, 5 Barfield Crs, Elizabeth West, Ph (08) 8255 1979 ☐ Gawler Cycles, 63 Murray St, Gawler, Ph (08) 8522 2343

2800km 9km out of Adelaide

2900km 25km before Blanchetown

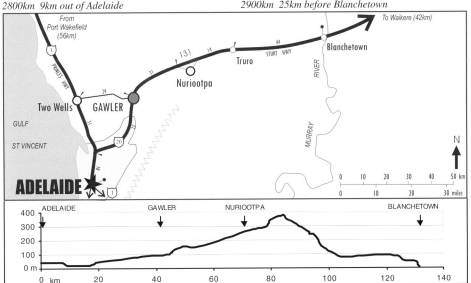

21 BLANCHETOWN TO REMARK

Blanchetown to:

Waikerie (Junction)	42km	c, m/h
Barmera	88km	c, m/h
Renmark (via Monash)	117km	c, m/h, i

For the next 350km the tour passes through towns on Australia's most important river; the Murray, and one of its tributaries the Murrumbidgee. The Murray flows for 2,600km from the Snowy Mountains in NSW to the Southern Ocean at Encounter Bay, SA. Along the way it supports the Snowy Mountains Hydroelectric Scheme and the Murrumbidgee and Murray Irrigation Areas. Murray water is even pumped as far west as the Eyre Peninsula.

Leaving Blanchetown the road crosses the river and heads directly across gently rolling farmland to Waikerie. Signs here indicate you are entering a Fruit Fly Exclusion Zone, and travellers are requested to deposit fruit into bins provided along the roadside.

Waikerie township is 2km off the highway but there is a fresh bread bakery at the turn-off so there may be no need to detour. After Waikerie the road is flat to gently rolling, passing through paddocks and citrus groves, with the river occasionally coming into view away to the left. The Murray follows a convoluted course here as it snakes across the plain. There are many lagoons and billabongs, and it's easy to imagine that Banjo Paterson had billabongs like these in mind when he wrote his famous poem about a swagman's ghost and a shady Coolabah tree in "Waltzing Matilda".

10km before Barmera the road skims Wachtels Lagoon, a sodden piece of earth with stark dead trees protruding, and crosses the Murray again. Barmera is a cross between a holiday resort and a retirement village, and sits next to a pretty little lake - Lake Bonney. In keeping with the areas rural roots the Australian Country Music Hall of Fame is here, resplendent with a giant sequinned guitar on the roof.

2km out of Bamera is Alt 20, a bypass avoiding the commercial centre of Berri, and saving 3km on the trip to Renmark. The bypass goes through the settlement of Monash before rejoining Route 20, 13km from Renmark.

Renmark sits on a bend in the Murray across from Bulyong Island National Park - a koala sanctuary. The town was established in 1887, and was the centre of the first irrigation project on the river. In the late 19th Century Renmark was unruly and had a reputation for its grog shops. Today, the town is a popular holiday destination with gracious wide streets, arts and craft shops, and paddle-steamers and house-boats moored at the riverbank.

The Chaffey Brothers

Two Canadian brothers, George and William (WB) Chaffey founded Renmark, and later Mildura. The Chaffeys were irrigation entrepreneurs who had successfully established fruit growing towns in the Southern Californian desert. Alfred Deakin, a Melbourne politician, later to become Australia's second Prime Minister, met George Chaffey in 1885 and invited him to inspect the Murray with a view to irrigation settlements. The brothers liked what they saw; a sun drenched climate and sandy loam soils, and decided to make the move, but a furore in the Victorian State Government prevented the release of land to them. The SA Government quickly stepped in and leased them 50,000 acres with an option on 200,000 more. Following a successful advertising campaign to attract settlers, the brothers established Renmark with the pumps and weirs required for irrigation. As the vines and citrus grew the Victorians interest was rekindled and they finally offered the brothers half a million acres at Mildura.

Like their Californian blueprint towns of Etawanda and Ontario, the Aussie towns

1956 The Olympic Games are held in Melbourne

were designed to be free from the sale of intoxicating liquor. In rural Australia this caused a few ruffles and the SA Government rapidly legislated a change. The settlements started promisingly but the financial crisis of 1893 caused the demand for citrus to drop and as settlers left rabbits moved in. The brother's irrigation trust went broke and they lost everything. George went back to California (borrowing the return fare) but WB stayed on, working as a hired labourer. He managed to keep 90 acres, which he faithfully tended, and convinced other growers to join him in a co-operative. He also gave up teetotalling and started a distillery. Things eventually recovered and the irrigation towns went on to great prosperity. WB's dried fruit co-op and distillery blossomed, eventually becoming the biggest in Australia, and he was elected Mildura's first mayor. Back in the U.S., George regrew his fortune too, built on water rights and banking. WB was buried in Mildura, while George was laid to rest near San Diego overlooking the Pacific.

Camping:
Waikerie Caravan Park, Peake Tce, <u>Waikerie</u>, Ph (08) 8541 2651, T$11 ☐ Lake Bonney Caravan Park, Lakeside Drv, <u>Barmera</u>, Ph (08) 8588 2234, T$11 ☐ Renmark Riverfront Caravan Park, Sturt Hwy, <u>Renmark</u>, Ph (08) 8586 6315, T$12 ☐ Riverbend Park, Sturt Hwy <u>Renmark</u>, Ph (08) 8595 5131, T$12 ☐ Others; <u>Waikerie</u>, <u>Barmera</u>, <u>Berri</u>, <u>Renmark</u>

Motel/Hotel:
Waikerie Hotel-Motel, 2 McCoy St, <u>Waikerie</u>, Ph (08) 8541 2999, S$40, D$50 ☐ Barmera Hotel Motel, Barwell Ave, <u>Barmera</u>, Ph (08) 8588 2111, S$30, D$40 ☐ Renmark Hotel-Motel, Murray Ave, <u>Renmark</u>, Ph (08) 8586 6755, S$50, D$60 ☐ Fountain Gardens Motel, Renmark Ave, <u>Renmark</u>, Ph (08) 8586 6899, S$50, D$60 ☐ Others; <u>Waikerie</u>, <u>Barmera</u>, <u>Berri</u>, <u>Renmark</u> (also a Hostel at <u>Berri</u>)

i:
Renmark/Paringa Visitor Centre, Murray Ave, <u>Renmark</u>, Ph (08) 8586 6704 ☐ Others; <u>Berri</u>

Bike Shop:
Nearest: Riverland Cycles, 22 Wilson St, <u>Berri</u>, Ph (08) 8582 1675

3000km 19km before Barmera

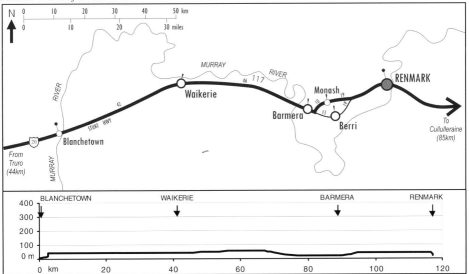

Renmark to:

Cullulleraine	85km c
Mildura	144km c, h, m/h, i, bike shop

After Renmark the route leaves the river and briefly skips across the top of a third state, Victoria, before rejoining the Murray at Mildura on the border with NSW. The road is flat to gently rolling.

On the outskirts of Renmark the road crosses a swing bridge over the Murray before climbing the opposite riverbank. Macadamia farms and vineyards line the road for a short distance then fade further from the river. 27km after Renmark is a service station and an arch across the road heralding Vic. The border also marks a time zone change with clocks going forward half an hour in NSW.

Cullulleraine, a dot on the map 85km from Renmark, has a service station and campground and is the only stop en route to Mildura. Watch out for magpies nesting along this stretch. During spring individual birds are prone to silently swoop down and flap past anything that trespasses into their territory. The key is not to lose concentration during one of these episodes and end up crashing or swerving into traffic. A consolation is that occasionally a dumb bird will dive bomb a truck.

Mildura is an even bigger tourist town than Renmark with caravan parks appearing 8km before downtown. The town derives its names from the Aboriginal for "red earth", and owes its prosperity to the Chaffey brothers irrigation scheme which turned the marginal sheep station here into fertile and productive land. The Murray River here also marks the border between Vic. and NSW - a psychological step closer to Sydney. At Mildura you can take a dinner cruise on a paddle steamer or hire a houseboat.

Australian Federation

The Vic./NSW state-line is marked by a sign in the middle of George Chaffey Bridge on the way out of Mildura. During colonial times a strong rivalry existed between NSW and Vic. One source of friction was the fact that towns this far from Sydney, although in NSW, generally did their trade with Melbourne which was geographically closer. Each of Australia's colonies had been established quite differently; with NSW a free-trade colony, while Vic. was strongly protectionist. A system of border tariffs existed between the colonies and there was the ridiculous situation of NSW and Vic. adopting different railway gauges (a situation that took 60 years to rectify).

A Governor who followed administrative instructions from Britain ran Australia's first colony, the penal settlement at Sydney in NSW. The first Governor was Arthur Phillip, Captain of the First Fleet. Other early NSW Governors included the immortal Captain Bligh (post-mutiny), and Major-General Lachlan Macquarie (who left behind many fine convict designed buildings). Subsequent Governors (or Lieutenant Governors) took up office; in Tasmania (originally Van Diemen's Land) in 1804, WA in 1828, SA in 1836, Vic. in 1851, and in Qld. in 1859.

By the early 1820's, authority over Australia's settlements was being handled by the Colonial Office in London. Run by the British Secretary of State and a permanent Under Secretary, this office had total control over all Australian matters (except constitutional issues, which went to the House of Commons). Still, many administrative matters were left to the individual Governors and as each settlement grew they developed their own trade policies, defence forces, and communications systems.

Although the name Australia had been in official use since 1824, the colonies were politically fractious and strongly parochial. By the 1850's there were calls for a united

Federation (the colonies grouped under a central authority, but independent in internal affairs). A Federal Council was elected in 1883, and by 1891 the Council had debated and agreed on a draft Constitution. In 1900, all the colonies agreed to the Constitution and it was presented to Britain, which passed "The Constitution Act To Constitute The Commonwealth Of Australia" in the House of Commons in July of that year. The Constitution established Australia as a nation, with a parliamentary system headed by the Queen (in a largely token role), and an upper Senate and lower House of Representatives.

Recently, there have been murmurings within Australia to discard the Queen as Head of State and become a republic - the most notable advocate was the recent Prime Minister Paul Keating who made the suggestion while in power. But there seems to be little groundswell for the idea at the moment and most Aussies are proud of their flag, which incorporates the Union Jack.

Camping:
Lake Cullulleraine Caravan Park, Sturt Hwy, Cullulleraine, Ph (03) 5028 2226, T$12 ☐ Big 4 Golden River Caravan Park, Flora Ave, Mildura, Ph (03) 5021 2299, T$15 ☐ Mildura & Deakin Holiday Park, Cnr 15th St & Deakin Ave, Mildura, Ph (03) 5023 0486, T$15 ☐ Others; Cullulleraine, Mildura

Hostel:
Mildura YHA, 154 Madden Ave, Mildura, Ph (03) 5023 1535, S$17, D$34 *(closing mid-2001)* ☐ Check with the Mildura Visitor Information Centre for other hostels which cater to seasonal workers

Motel/Hotel:
Kar-rama Motor Inn, 153 Deakin Ave, Mildura, Ph (03) 5023 4221, S$42, D$47 ☐ 7th Street Motel, 153 7th St, Mildura, Ph (03) 5023 1796, S$41, D$50 ☐ Others; Mildura

i:
Mildura Visitor Information Centre, 180 Deakin Ave, Mildura, Ph (03) 5021 4424

Bike Shops:
Mildura Cycles, 154 Ninth St, Mildura, Ph (03) 5021 1584 ☐ Hodgson Cycles & Hobbies, 106 Pine Ave, Mildura, Ph (03) 5023 6041 ☐ Others; Mildura

3100km 37km before Cullulleraine

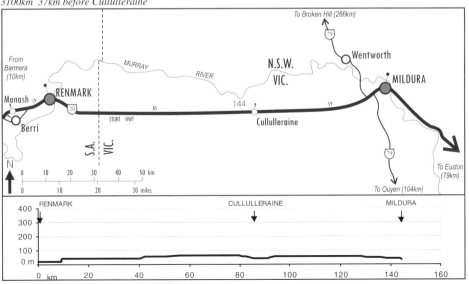

MILDURA

This small city, with a population of about 25,000 has grown up around the fruit and nut growing industries made possible by the Chaffey brothers irrigation scheme. A statue of **WB Chaffey**, the town's first mayor, is in Deakin Street. If you want to get out onto Australia's greatest river, restored **paddle steamers** leave from the wharf at the end of Deakin St for cruises. Some offer lunch or dinner accompanied by live music.

There is a good walk along the Mildura river bank; through **Jaycee Park** past the **Old Power House** and **Pumping Station**, and into **Rio Vista Park** with its **Historical Display** and the nearby **Mildura Arts Centre**, which incorporates **Rio Vista** the preserved homestead of the Chaffey brothers. At the western end of Rio Vista Park is **Lock 11**, one of the 26 locks on the river, which control its flow. Lock 11 doubles as a foot bridge over to **Lock Island**, a koala and wildlife sanctuary in the middle of the river. For those wanting to get physical on the water there are a number of water sports available - fishing, kayaking, water skiing, etc (enquire at the Visitors Centre).

Also in Mildura is **Pioneer Cottage** on Hunter Street (a reconstruction of early Sunraysia life). The locals are also pretty proud of the bar at the Workingman's Club on Deakin St - it's reputedly the longest in the world.

Mildura has a busy festival schedule throughout the year including sports, art and culture, and food and wine events. In addition there are bicycle races and motorcycle rallies that pass through, paddle boat races, wildflower and country music festivals, and a unique event called "The Great Australian Vanilla Slice Triumph".

Outside Mildura there are **wineries** to tour and several **National Parks** worth a visit (some incorporating large tracts of mallee country).

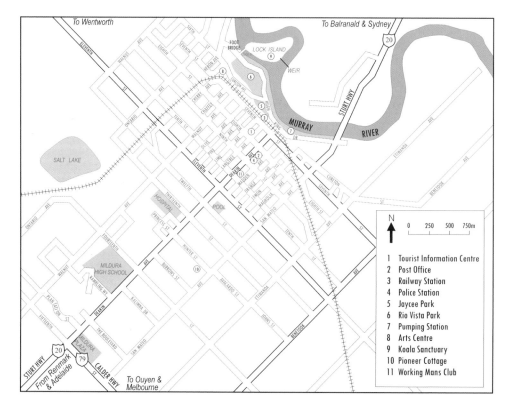

1966 Joern Utzon, the Danish architect who designed the Sydney Opera House, leaves mid-construction after disagreements with the NSW State Governerment

The Murray River near Mildura

MILDURA TO BALRANALD

Mildura to:

Euston	79km c, m/h
Balranald	158km c, m/h

The road out of Mildura passes orchards and vineyards before crossing flat to gently rolling scrub country to Euston. Across the river from Euston is the larger town of Robinvale, back in Vic., which developed as a returning soldier settlement after World War II. Both towns have accommodation. The road touches the Murray for the last time at Euston, before crossing the delightfully named Deadman Plain to Balranald.

Just past Euston the road passes two small lakes (Dry Lake and Lake Benanee), then the flat expanse of Deadman Plain, before wheat fields reappear near Balranald. Old wooden homes, most in need of a coat of paint, line Balranald's main street - testament to a time when business was better in the town (the first telephone in Australia was installed on a homestead near here by a nephew of Alexander Graham Bell). The town campground is on a shady bend of the Murrumbidgee River. Signs around the camping area warn that the tall gums occasionally, spontaneously, drop branches.

The Burke and Wills Expedition

Robert Burke stayed in Balranald on 17 September 1860 at the start of his successful, but ultimately fatal, attempt to traverse Australia south to north. In the 1850's the huge central deserts of the continent were still unexplored and the SA Government offered £2,000 for the first person to undertake a crossing. Robert Burke, a 39-year-old Irishman with little experience in the Outback, was chosen by the Victorian Expedition Committee to lead an attempt from Melbourne. At the same time, John Stuart a hardened desert explorer was setting off from Adelaide to claim the prize for SA. Burke's team was lavishly equipped and included 24 camels specially imported from India. On the day of departure 10,000 people turned out to farewell the expeditioners.

After several toasts to Queen Victoria had been made and an escaped camel rounded up, the expedition began but by the time he reached Balranald, Burke was having problems. Here the team foreman quarrelled with Burke over his autocratic leadership and was fired - others departed soon afterwards. In an effort to make haste Burke divided the expedition and pushed on with an advance party to Cooper Creek, in southern Qld. After waiting here for 5 weeks the main party had still not arrived and Burke decided to split his team again.

Leaving 4 men at the Cooper Creek depot, with instructions to wait for them at least 3 months, Burke, his second in command William Wills, and 2 others; John King, and Charles Gray - set off northwards for the Gulf of Carpentaria. After 2 arduous months they noticed their tea, made with river water, was salty and 3 days later they reached the swampy northern coast, although they never saw the open ocean. Growing gradually weaker on the return journey Gray was unable to continue walking and had to be strapped to a camel. Under worsening privations they were forced eat their horses and eventually Gray passed away.

Meanwhile the dawdling main party had still not relieved the Cooper Creek camp and since Burke was now a month overdue, the worst was feared and it was decided to abandon the depot. It was dusk when Burke, Wills, and King finally crawled back into Cooper Creek, 4 months after leaving - only to find the others had departed 7 hours earlier. The word "DIG" was freshly blazed into a Coolabah tree and on digging they found food and a letter indicating the party had departed southward that morning with camels and horses in "good working order". Incredibly they had taken two thirds of the food with them for the return journey, leaving insufficient supplies for Burke, Wills and King to return south.

Burke was crestfallen, knowing he would never be able to catch his companions' fresh mounts (in fact these animals were so unfit from sitting around for 4 months that they were not in "good working order" at all, and the party was camped only 20km from Burke that night).

After 3 days at the depot Burke buried his diaries under the DIG tree and the 3 men set off westward in an attempt to make the nearest cattle station at Mt Hopeless. Meanwhile, the men who had deserted the depot had had second thoughts while heading home, and to reassure themselves two of them rode back to check the depot one last time. They tied their horses to the DIG tree, where Burke's diaries and letter of intentions were buried below and briefly surveyed the campsite. Seeing no sign of life or fresh marks on the Coolabah tree they didn't bother to check the cache below and set off towards Melbourne again.

Burke, Wills, and King made it 50km before their two remaining camels died and they were stranded. They lived for a while off camel meat and desert plants but gradually grew weaker. Burke and Wills both passed away in the desert but King was found by friendly Aborigines and was eventually located by a search party 3 months later.

As if this tragic series of mix-ups wasn't enough, a rider had been dispatched from Melbourne early on in the saga carrying the message that Stuart's crossing had been unsuccessful and there was now no urgency - the message never reached Cooper Creek.

Camping:
Riverfront Caravan Park, 27 Murray Tce, Euston, Ph (03) 5026 1543, T$10 ☐ Balranald Caravan Park, 60 Court St, Balranald, Ph (03) 5020 1321, T$9 ☐ Others; Robinvale

Motel/Hotel:
Euston Motel, Sturt Hwy, Euston, Ph (03) 5026 3806, S$55, D$65 ☐ Sturt Motel, 32 River St, Balranald, Ph (03) 5020 1309, S$50, D$58 ☐ Balranald Motor Inn, 154 Market St, Balranald, Ph (03) 5020 1104, S$75, D$78 ☐ Others; Robinvale, Balranald

3200km 5km past Mildura

3300km 60km before Balranald

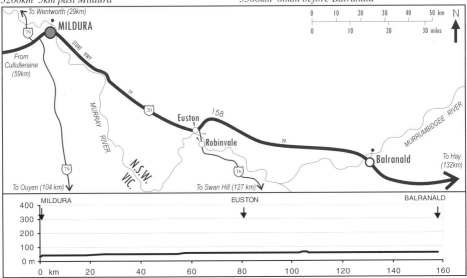

Balranald to:

Hay   132km c, m/h, i

The stretch between Balranald and Hay is a good example of the remote regions that still exist in inland NSW. The road crosses the Hay Plains for 132km without passing a single service station or shop. The road is flat but unprotected and the ease of the ride is dictated by the wind.

The highway out of Balranald crosses the Murrumbidgee and passes an billboard with the buoying message "Next McDonald's 482km". The road has a wide shoulder and for most of the stage crosses a shrub-covered plain dotted with occasional stands of trees. Towards Hay the effects of irrigation from the Murrumbigee River become apparent as huge wheat fields appear. Tractors, towing sprinklers hundreds of meters wide, taxi up and down the fields and stray wheat grows along the roadside.

Three highways: The Cobb, The Sturt, and The Mid-Western congregate at the roundabout at the edge of Hay. From here a steel bridge takes you across the Murrumbigee and up the main street, Lachlan St. The town grew up as a river crossing for sheep and is still a commercial centre for the surrounding pastoral area. Lachlan St has solid stone buildings, many from last century, carefully restored in their original "heritage" colours and an original Cobb & Co. stage coach, one of the ones that travelled the Cobb Highway back in the 1800's is on display. One of the oldest buildings in Hay is the grim looking goal (jail), built in 1878. It finally closed in 1973 and is now the town museum. The early days of Hay, and nearby Booligal, were the focus of a disparaging poem by Australia's most famous bush ballader - Banjo Paterson.

Hay and Hell Booligal

v.1
'You come and see me, boys, ' he said;
'You'll find a welcome and a bed
   And whiskey any time you call;
Although our township hasn't got
The name of quite a lively spot -
   You see, I live in Booligal.

v.2
'And people have an awful down
Upon the district and the town -
   Which worse than Hell itself the call;
In fact, the saying far and wide
Along the Riverina side
   Is "Hay and Hell and Booligal".

v.3
'No doubt it suits 'em very well
To say its worse than Hay or Hell
   But don't you heed their talk at all;
Of course, there's heat - no one denies -
And sand and dust and stacks of flies,
   And rabbits, too, at Booligal.

v.4
'But such a pleasant, quiet place -
You never see a stranger's face;
   They hardly ever care to call;
The drovers mostly pass it by -
They reckon that they'd rather die
   Than spend the night in Booligal.

v.5
'The big mosquitoes frighten some -
You'll lie awake to hear 'em hum -
   And snakes about the township crawl;
But shearers, when they get their cheque,
They never come along and wreck
   The blessed town of Booligal.

v.6
'But down to Hay the shearers come
And fill themselves with fighting-rum,
   And chase blue devils up the wall,
And fight the snaggers every day,
Until there is the deuce to pay -
   There's none of that in Booligal.

v.7
'Of course, there isn't much to see -
The billiard-table used to be
   The great attraction for us all,
Until some careless, drunken curs
Got sleeping on it in their spurs,
   And ruined it, in Booligal.

v.8
'Just now there is a howling drought
That pretty near has starved us out -
   It never seems to rain at all;
But, if there *should* come any rain,
You couldn't cross the black-soil plain -
   You'd have to stop in Booligal.'

v.9   *'We'd have to stop!'* With bated breath
We prayed that both in life and death
Our fate in other lines might fall:
'Oh, send us to our just reward
In Hay or Hell, but gracious Lord,
Deliver us from Booligal!'.

Although his name conjures up the image of an Outback swagman, AB (Banjo) Paterson worked most of his life in Sydney. His love for the bush came from growing up on the family station near Orange NSW, before being sent to Sydney Grammar at age 10. He trained as a solicitor, then worked as a law clerk, a war correspondent (in the Boer War), and a journalist, often writing for *The Bulletin*. Paterson had a poetic duel in *The Bulletin* with another other famous Outback poet; Henry Lawson, with Lawson accusing Banjo of romanticising bush life (the parrying back and forth in verse no doubt assisting circulation). Both Lawson and Paterson captured images of the bush that Australians were sympathetic with. Paterson's most famous verse, Waltzing Matilda, has become Australia's unofficial national anthem - a fine tribute to the country's greatest bush poet.

Camping:
Hay Caravan Park, Moama St (Sturt Hwy), Hay, Ph (02) 6993 1415, T$10 ☐ Hay Plains Holiday Park, 4 Naylor St, Hay, Ph (02) 6993 1875, T$10

Motel/Hotel:
New Crown Hotel-Motel, 117 Lachlan St, Hay, Ph (02) 6993 1600, S$35, D$45 ☐ Bidgee Motor Inn, 74 Lachlan St, Hay, Ph (02) 6993 2260, S$48, D$54 ☐ Motel Hay, Cnr Sturt Hwy & Cobb Hwy, Hay, Ph (02) 6993 1804, S$50, D$55 ☐ Others; Hay

i:
Hay Tourist and Amenities Centre, 407 Moppett St, Hay, Ph (02) 6993 4045

3400km 95km before Hay

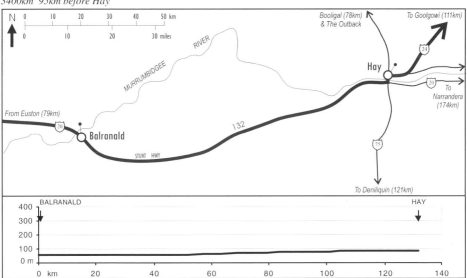

25 HAY TO GOOLGOWI

Hay to:

Goolgowi   111km c, m/h

At the northern end of Hay's main street is the start of the Mid-Western Highway - only 733km to Sydney. The Mid-Western and Sturt Highways are about the same distance to Sydney, but this tour takes the Mid-Western to pass through the beautiful Blue Mountains and avoid some of the heavy Melbourne to Sydney traffic. The road is flat all the way to Goolgowi.

5km out of Hay there is a tree that Charles Sturt reportedly blazed when he passed here in 1830, on his journey to the mouth of the Murray. Leaving Hay the road quickly rejoins the Hay Plain, with only a few patches of land opened up for cereal crops by irrigation. Even in such open country there is still an abundance of wildlife - mournfully marked by unrecognisable leathery bundles smoothed onto road.

Gunbar is labelled on some maps between Hay and Goolgowi, but it's only a meeting of dirt roads where the highway bends eastward for the final 32km into Goolgowi.

Goolgowi is a tiny town at the junction of the Mid-Western Highway and the Kidman Way. A plaque on the local council building proudly displays the settlement's "Top Town - Category A, Youth and Water Scheme Winner" credentials, and you get the feeling these people are proud of their little piece of Australia. There is no commercial campground in town, however the council provides a field for camping with a simple ablution block and honesty box. The site is near the town's rugby league club and is signposted.

The Kidman Way heading north-south through Goolgowi is in reference to Sir Sidney Kidman, who had a string of cattle stations running from the heart of NSW to Vic., and another set of properties in central Australia and northern SA. Kidman was a self-made man who started work at 13 as a bush cook's assistant. By the time he was a teenager he was guiding parties into the Outback in search of grazing country, and breeding horses for the British Army to use in India. As his property empire grew he developed a system of moving sheep and cattle between his farms to avoid water shortages and maximise feed. Kidman, also known as "The Cattle King", ended up owning property greater in area than the state of Victoria, and he was able to move his stock directly to all major points-of-sale without the animals leaving his holdings. His descendants still run Anna Creek station in SA, a property the size of Belgium.

The White Australia Policy

Before the 1970's your best bet for coming to live in Australia was to be European. That's because up until the 70's, successive Governments used so-called "White Australia" immigration policies to restrict the inflow of people from non-European countries. The result was that 80% of new settlers came from the UK or Europe.

The origins of the policy date from 1855 when resentment against the growing number of Chinese miners on the Buckland goldfield in Vic. resulted in the Chinese being driven from the area and their tents burned. The same thing happened in 1860 at the Lambing Flat goldfield in NSW when a rioting mob attacked and destroyed a Chinese camp, forcing them off the field. When they dared to return they were attacked again, along with their families, by posses welding pick handles. These incidents, spurred by the miner's fears of a flood of cheap Asian labour, lead to restrictions being placed on Chinese immigration.

In the 1860's and 70's, large numbers of Pacific Islanders were bought to Australia (often by kidnapping or trickery) by "blackbirders" to work the Qld. sugarcane

1971 Nic Roeg's movie "Walkabout" is released

plantations. Again resentment brewed among Australian workers about the importation of labour, and controls were introduced. When an economic depression loomed in the 1890's many Islanders were shipped back to their homelands, and by 1901 an Immigration Restriction Act was in place.

With many fearful of a crowded Asia spilling over into empty Australia, the reasons behind the White Australia policies were often more social or political than economic. Australia's second Prime Minister, Alfred Deakin, stated in support of immigration controls, that the unity of Australia was nothing if it did not imply a united race.

Following World War II a gradual softening of policies took place with certain non-European refugees and war brides being allowed in. The term "White Australia Policy" was officially removed from Government documents by 1945, but it was Harold Holt's 1966 Government that essentially signalled the end of active discrimination (although the ethnic mix of the intake was still controlled).

Subsequent Governments made non-European immigration more achievable and as Asia became a favoured trading partner Asian immigration increased, reaching 50% of the annual intake for the first time in 1990.

Australia was recently embroiled in a new race debate, when a controversial Independent Member of Parliament, Pauline Hanson, once again called for strict controls on Asian immigration, tapping into the fears of a certain segment of the electorate.

Camping:
Goolgowi Council Caravan Park, Goolgowi, Ph (02) 6965 1331, T$7

Motel/Hotel:
Highway Motel, Mid-Western Hwy, Goolgowi, Ph (02) 6965 1445, S$55, D$66

3500km Leaving Hay

3600km 8km before Goolgowi

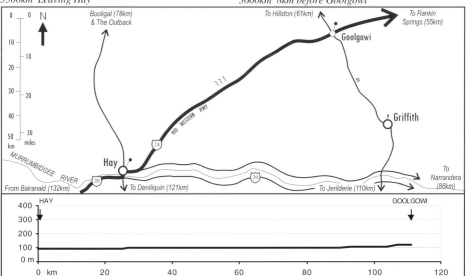

1972 Aboriginal rights protestors set up a camp on Parliament grounds in Canberra to draw attention to their cause. Police eventually evict them

103

Goolgowi to:

Rankins Springs	55km	m/h
Weethalle	91km	m/h
West Wyalong	147km	c, m/h, i

After Goolgowi the barren Hay Plains are just a memory. The highway passes through truly green countryside with fields of wheat and paddocks of grazing sheep. The road gradually climbs the wooded spine of Tabbita Ridge before sweeping down through a gap in the rocks to the pretty village of Rankins Springs. The grocery store here is run by a burly, once highflying, entrepreneur from Melbourne who gave up the stress of city-life and escaped to the country. The towns pride is shown in its little park adorned with a pergola and flowerbeds. Rankins Springs is named after Arthur Rankin, one of the first settlers in the area.

Past Rankins Springs the highway is gently rolling and enters the "Shire of Bland". The area is named after William Bland a doctor, and an altogether interesting character, who was transported to Sydney as a convict after killing a man in a duel in Bombay. He was put in charge of Sydney's lunatic asylum before being pardoned and setting up Australia's first private practice. He was in goal again for 12 months after publishing a libellous verse against Governor Macquarie, before becoming instrumental in founding Sydney Grammar School, opening a dispensary for the poor, and joining the Legislative Council of the colony. His convict background was used by some to thwart his advance but the first settlers here regarded him highly, naming the region after him.

The road to Weethalle passes pretty farmland flanked by trees full of chattering birds. Weethalle has a hotel, service station and several shops. It's another 56km to West Wyalong, the first town of any size since Hay.

The main street of West Wyalong is a bit crooked due to a lack of surveying during the 1893 gold rush and some tree stumps that the road was hastily bent around. Shops sprung up before it could be straightened so that's the way it has stayed. One of the older houses in the main street is the local museum - a jumble of interesting artefacts, antiques and junk. Despite the clutter, or perhaps because of it, it gives a good sense of the town's history. One item, tucked away in the back, and interesting for some inexplicable reason, is a set of "sheep's boots" - the matting of golden spinifex that collects around the shanks of stray sheep as they wander the countryside.

West Wyalong has a good range of accommodation and services (although no bike shop). There is a campground on the way into town, and one in the centre of town between Operator and Perseverance St's. West Wyalong is Australia's main producer of eucalyptus oil.

West Wyalong's Gold

In 1833, farmers seeking pasture settled the West Wyalong area. The district developed slowly until one day in September 1893 when Joseph Neeld chipped away at a quartz vein on his property and found gold. Within a year there were over 10,000 diggers in the area and the State Government set to work laying out the town of Wyalong to service the influx. The miners however had no desire to relocate from their diggings, and their camp, which was in fact much larger than the new Wyalong, was surreptitiously named West Wyalong and grew into the dominant town.

The areas gold was locked in narrow north-northeast trending quartz reefs, formed from hot, gold bearing, fluids which pushed upward from a body of buried magma. In order to win the gold the miners had to sink deep shafts and branch out horizontally along

1973 Patrick White wins the Nobel Prize for literature after penning books such as "Tree of Man" and "Voss", both describing the Australian Outback.

the veins as far as possible. The Mid-Western Highway crosses the richest reef, the Mallee Bull, near Boundary Rd, half way between West Wyalong and Wyalong. Early last century ore was being hoisted to the surface along this reef from shafts with names like Neeld's, True Blue, Lady Hampden, and the deepest at 300m; the Brilliant Shaft. The ore averaged about 55 grams of gold per ton - an impressive concentration (that's a gold cube 1.4cm square from a load of rock about 75cm x 75cm x 75cm).

Gradually as the veins pinched out or became too deep to follow, the mining slowed and by the 1920's activity at West Wyalong had ceased. The old mine tailings were briefly reworked in the 1930's when cyanide was used to recover gold missed the first time around, but following this the town settled back into its roll as a rural support centre.

Mining might not be at an end in West Wyalong though, companies still have leases on land to the north and south of the town, and a drilling program is underway to assess the feasibility of establishing new gold and copper operations.

Camping:
Ace Caravan Park, Cnr Newell and Mid-Western Hwys, West Wyalong, Ph (02) 6972 3061, T$10 ☐ West Wyalong Caravan Park, 60 Main St, West Wyalong, Ph (02) 6972 3133, T$8

281 Neeld St, West Wyalong, Ph (02) 6972 2777, S$40, D$44 ☐ Charles Sturt Motor Inn, Newell Hwy, West Wyalong, Ph (02) 6972 2422, S$50, D$60 ☐ Others; West Wyalong

Motel/Hotel:
Rankins Springs Boomerang Motel, Boomerang St, Rankins Springs, Ph (02) 6966 1240, S$38, D$50 ☐ Travellers Rest Motel, Mid-Western Hwy, Weethalle, Ph (02) 6975 6193, S$37, D$46 ☐ Central Motel,

i:
Tourist Information - The Tourist Train, McCann Pk, Main St, West Wyalong, Ph (02) 6972 3645

3700km 1km before Weethale

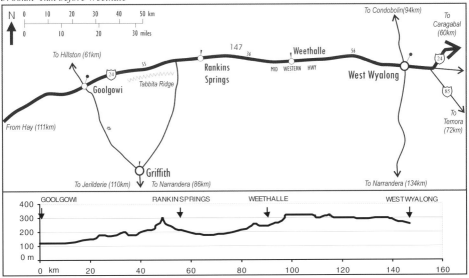

WEST WYALONG TO COWRA

West Wyalong to:

Marsden (Intersection)	37km
Caragabal	60km m/h
Grenfell	104km c, m/h, i
Cowra	159km c, m/h, i, bike shop

For 37km after West Wyalong the Mid-Western Highway is joined by traffic from the Newell Highway, a route between Brisbane and Melbourne, and the road is busy. At Marsden (an intersection) the Mid-Western Highway splits off and heads east for Sydney.

The road gently rolls across a rumpled countryside of yellow and green canola and wheat fields. 60km from West Wyalong is Caragabal - a country village with a pub, a few stores, and like most Australian towns, a war memorial in the main street. About 30km after Caragabal the terrain becomes rolling and just before the town of Grenfell there is a stiff climb past the town's reservoir perched on a hill. Below, a prosperous little town is spread out with the dark green Wedden Mountains as a back drop to the south. In the 1850's and 60's these mountains were a stronghold for bushrangers who repeatedly held-up travellers in the area. After gold was discovered here in 1866 a group of outlaws swept into town, killed the gold commissioner JG Grenfell, and high-tailed it back to the mountains. When the town was proclaimed it was named in honour of the murdered gold agent. Grenfell's old buildings have thoughtfully been retained in the main street, along with a monument to Henry Lawson, a famous poet born in a tent on the goldfields here.

After Grenfell the highway gradually becomes hilly. About 20km before Cowra the road reaches a hilltop overlooking the Lachlan River with Cowra in the distance. The last 20km into town are downhill or flat. The highway crosses the Lachlan and heads up Cowra's main street (there is a campground on the banks of the river, just after the bridge into town). Cowra was the site of a POW camp during World War II. Japanese prisoners imprisoned here staged a mass breakout in 1944 and a large number of prisoners and several guards were killed. Because of the town's history, Cowra has made a real effort to establish Australian-Japanese ties, including the building of a Japanese cultural centre and garden, and every October hosting "Sakura Matsuri" (Cherry Blossom Festival).

Cowra POW Camp Breakout

Nestled in the rolling hills of the Lachlan Valley in August 1944 was the No. 12 POW Camp at Cowra. It was a circular camp fenced into four quarters holding Italian prisoners in two quarters, Korean, Formosan Island, and Japanese officers in another quarter, and in the last quarter, Camp B, eleven hundred Japanese soldiers. In the early morning hours of August the 5th the Japanese prisoners in Camp B staged the largest prisoner escape in British military history. It was also a suicidal scheme doomed to fail.

The previous day the Camp B leader had been informed that a number of prisoners were to be transferred to the POW Camp at Hay. Some of the inmates had grumbled but there was nothing to indicate what would take place a few hours later. For the guards, every other night watch at the camp had been quiet, but at 1:30am this morning they faced 1,100 prisoners who, at a prearranged call, came yelling and screaming out of their torched huts. Wearing clothing padded with blankets and carrying a selection of improvised clubs and knives, they charged the barbed wire fences in three places. Jolted into activity the guards manning machine gun posts, and others with rifles, let loose showers of bullets along the fence lines. The Japanese suffered terrible losses but by shear numbers eventually managed to break through the wire. They clubbed and stabbed to death guards still manning a machine gun and a rifleman, then fled into the countryside.

1975 A crisis occurs when the Government and opposition stalemate over a Supply Bill. The Governor-General steps in and controversially dismisses the PM Gough Whitlam

Over the next 9 days Australia's biggest manhunt took place and all the prisoners were rounded up. Many committed suicide rather than surrendering; the Sydney Daily Telegraph reporting two prisoners had even lain in the path of an on-coming train. Others were shot by as they attempted raids on local farms. The final death toll was 231 Japanese and 4 Australians. The tragic events had their origins in the Imperial Japanese Army's ancient code of honour, in which a soldier became a "living dead" completely without honour if he was taken prisoner. This psyche resulted in the appalling treatment of Allied POW's by the Japanese during the war and because of this Australia initially censored details of the Cowra breakout, fearing reprisals against Australian prisoners by the Japanese who were not signatories to the Geneva Convention on the treatment of POW's.

Following the bitterness of the war, Cowra embraced a spirit of reconciliation and the town now has an avenue of cherry trees running between the POW camp site and the war graves cemetery, each tree sponsored by a Japanese and an Australian child.

Camping:
Grenfell Caravan Park, 10 Grafton St, Grenfell, Ph (02) 6343 1194, T$12 ▢ Cowra Caravan Park, Lachlan St, Cowra, Ph (02) 6342 1058, T$10 ▢ The Pines Caravan Park, Grenfell Rd, Cowra, Ph (02) 6342 1850, T$11 ▢ Others; Cowra

Motel/Hotel:
Royal Hotel, Wyalong St, Caragabal, Ph (02) 6347 5336, S$15, D$25 ▢ Grenfell Motel, 84 Main St, Grenfell, Ph (063) 43 1333, S$41, D$50 ▢ Cowra Motor Inn, 3 Macquarie St, Cowra, Ph (02) 6342

2011, S$42, D$52 ▢ Cowra Crest Motel, 133 Kendal St, Cowra, Ph (02) 6342 2799, S$49, D$58 ▢ Others; Grenfell, Cowra

i:
Grenfell Visitor Information Centre, 68 Main St, Grenfell, Ph (02) 6343 1612 ▢ Cowra Visitor Information Centre, Mid-Western Hwy, Cowra, Ph (02) 6342 4333

Bike Shop:
Time 4 Fitness, 24 Macquarie St, Cowra, Ph (02) 6342 4292

3800km 40km past West Wyalong

3900km 20km before Cowra

28 COWRA TO BATHURST

Cowra to:

Mandurama	51km	m/h
Blayney	70km	c, m/h
Bathurst	108km	c, m/h, i, bike shop

This is a hilly section. Between Cowra and Bathurst the road climbs the foothills leading up to the Blue Mountains, and as you finally get closer to Sydney the number of towns en route, and the traffic increases.

Lyndhurst has a service station and store. 4km further on at Mandurama there is a more substantial set of shops. With the higher traffic flows towards Sydney the highway gets a real hammering and the road surface around Mandurama is particularly bad. The seal is broken in places and pushed up into ridges in others, and riding requires constant attention.

Blayney, sitting in the Central Tablelands, is a mid-sized agricultural town of 2,500 with a decent set of shops. The hills continue after Blayney, including a climb past Fitzgerald Mountain near Bathurst.

On the way into Bathurst the road passes Mount Panorama where the town's famous touring car race is held every year (if you arrive in October during the "Great Race" without booking ahead don't expect to find accommodation). Bathurst is the oldest inland town in Australia, built after a road had finally been forged through the Blue Mountains in 1815. The flaggy bluffs of these mountains, although not high in altitude, presented a formidable barrier to the first settlers in Sydney, and what was westward remained a mystery until Gregory Blaxland managed a crossing in 1813.

At least seven previous expeditions had failed before Blaxland's effort. They all tried following valleys into the mountains before being turned back by sheer cliff faces. Blaxland's theory was to follow the ridges rather than the valleys, and his expedition, comprising William Lawson, William Wentworth, and 4 convicts, was the first to see the fertile Western Plains. As a reward Blaxland, Lawson, and Wentworth were each granted 1,000 acres in the "new country". Lawson was the first to drive stock over the mountains and take up land on the Campbell River, near the future site of Bathurst.

Governor Macquarie travelled the newly completed road in 1815 and selected the site for a new town, naming it after Earl Bathurst, the British Secretary of State for the Colonies. Bathurst grew firstly as an agricultural centre then in 1851 its wealth was boosted by the discovery nearby of the first economically viable gold in the colony. This town was also the starting point for many of Australia's great explorers: Evans, Oxley, Cunningham, Sturt, and Mitchell.

As a reminder of how recent European settlement is in this country, the first peel of bells to be heard in Australia was rung from the Bathurst Cathedral in 1855. Today the pioneering families of Bathurst are remembered on plaques at a memorial beside the Macquarie River, each plaque with a story of where the settlers arrived from and what became of them. Other attractions in the town include the original 1817 Government House, a good nature reserve at Mt Panorama with informative trails, and the home of the city's most famous son Ben Chiefly, Prime Minister from 1945-1949.

Petrolheads Paradise

The name Bathurst means one thing to Australian sports fans - motor racing. Every October since 1960 a touring car race has been staged in Bathurst. The "Bathurst 1,000" is a religious event among motor-sport followers, with tens of thousands making the pilgrimage to the Mount Panorama circuit to watch souped up versions of production

1978 A bomb blast outside the Sydney Hilton, venue of a Heads of Government Meeting, kills two passersby

cars missile around the 6.2km track at 260km/hr. The fans are fiercely bipartisan, supporting either the Fords or the Holdens, and as the drama of the race unfolds the real contest is which V8 will prevail - the Falcon (Ford) or the Commodore (Holden). Regardless of loyalties, for the past 30 years the demi-god of Bathurst has been Peter Brock ("Peter Perfect" to his fans) who won a record 9 Bathursts before his retirement in 1997. Brock, and the other winners of The Great Race are immortalised on plaques embedded in the pavement in the main street. Once the race is over Mt. Panorama reverts to a public road and you can negotiate the twisting track for yourself - at 60km/hr.

Camping:
Blayney Caravan Park, Quamby Pl, <u>Blayney</u>, Ph (02) 6368 2799, T$7 ☐ Bathurst Big 4 Tourist Park, Sydney Rd, Kelso (4km E of Bathurst), <u>Bathurst</u>, Ph (02) 6331 8286, T$10

Motel/Hotel:
Royal Hotel, Main St, <u>Lyndhurst</u>, Ph (02) 6367 5024, S$18, D$35 ☐ Sunny Ridge Country Guest House, Canowindra Rd, <u>Mandurama</u>, Ph (02) 6367 5092, D$120 ☐ Royal Hotel, Belubula St, <u>Carcoar</u>, Ph (02) 6367 3009, S$20, D$38 ☐ Blayney Goldfields Motor Inn, 48 Martha St, <u>Blayney</u>, Ph (02) 6368 2000, S$55, D$65, ☐ Abercrombie Motor Inn, 362 Stewart St (Mid-Western Hwy), <u>Bathurst</u>, Ph (02) 6331 1077,

S$48, D$58 ☐ Bathurst Motor Inn, 87 Durham St, <u>Bathurst</u>, Ph (02) 6331 2222 or 1 800 043 321, S$50, D$65 ☐ Country Lodge Motor Inn, 145 William St, <u>Bathurst</u>, Ph (02) 6331 4888, S$65, D$75 ☐ Others; <u>Mandurama</u>, <u>Blayney</u>, <u>Bathurst</u>

i:
The Bathurst Visitors Centre, 28 William Street, <u>Bathurst</u>, Ph (02) 6332 1444

Bike Shops:
Winning Edge Cycles, 88 Durham St, <u>Bathurst</u>, Ph (02) 6332 4025 ☐ Pets & Pedals, 221 Russell St, <u>Bathurst</u>, Ph (02) 6331 4601 ☐ Toyworld Bathurst, 76 George St, <u>Bathurst</u>, Ph (02) 6334 3144

4000km 3km before Blayney

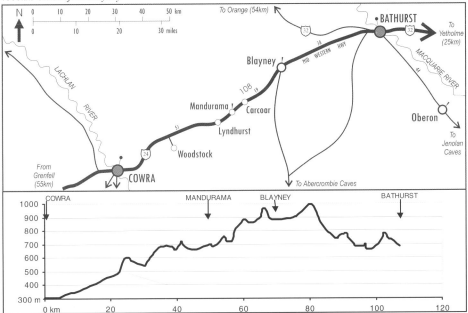

29 BATHURST TO KATOOMBA

Bathhurst to:

Lithgow	66km	c, m/h, i
Mount Victoria	88km	m/h
Blackheath	94km	c, m/h, i
Katoomba	106km	c, h, m/h, i, bike shop

This is the most topographic section of the tour. Almost immediately out of Bathurst the road starts climbing in a series of moderate to steep hills as the road ascends the Blue Mountains - a range that was not crossed for the first 25 years of European settlement.

About 25km from Bathurst a sign next to a service station indicates "Yetholme Crest 1,180m". The road drops briefly then rolls along, with some tough hill climbs, to another sign; "Great Dividing Range 1,150m". The highway then sweeps down, past the huge smoking stack of the Mt Piper power station into Lithgow. The centre of town is 2km off the highway. A mine here supplied coal to the Department of State Railways until torrential rains in 1964 flooded the underground workings and the mine was abandoned. The town is famous for its zigzag railway, where trains descended the Blue Mountains in a series of tight switchbacks until tunnels made the system redundant in 1910.

Past Lithgow the traffic increases noticeably and the road surface is either very good with a wide smooth shoulder, or very bad with little shoulder and deformed asphalt bulges. 11km past Lithgow is the historic settlement of Hartley, one of the first towns built on the Western Plains and now partially restored. 6km further on is Little Hartley (although both Hartleys are now little) at the foot of Victoria Pass. The Pass is a towering roadway built out of sandstone blocks by convict labour. The walls twist up into the clouds past lofty bluffs like a stairway to heaven, and it's a tough 3km climb in low gear. It is sobering to think of the 200 chained convicts who spent two years building this Pass block by block. At the top you are truly in the Blue Mountains where it's often several degrees cooler and considerably wetter than the plains below.

The road crests a plateau and gently rolls through eucalypt bush dotted with attractive houses. Between Blackheath and Katoomba is a heavily fortified tree, which Blaxland reputedly marked during that first crossing of the Blue Mountains in 1813. The tree is in a sad state. The top was cut off in the early 1900's and its dusty trunk doesn't have a hint of greenery.

Katoomba is a favourite get-away for Sydney-siders and a popular tourist destination (i.e. it's expensive). At the end of Lurline St is a lookout over the much-photographed Three Sisters rock formation and a fantastic, but precipitous, walking track into the valley below.

Bush Fires

Bush fires are a hazard in the leafy suburbs of many Australian towns and cities (including Sydney), and the settlements of the Blue Mountains are no exception. Lithgow, the little city between Bathurst and Katoomba suffered its worst fires in living memory in December 1997. A fiery ring descended the hills around the town, and front-page pictures in national newspapers showed Lithgow surrounded by sheets of flame. Miraculously, firefighters held the flames at the town's doorstep, although two firemen died in the effort.

Advice from the Bush Fires Board of Western Australia on what to expect if caught in your home during a bush fire makes for frightening reading... "Expect showers of sparks and embers before the main fire front approaches"... and ... "Expect strong winds and heavy smoke which will make it dark"... and the understatement ... "The fire will generate a very loud noise level which may be traumatic". Unlucky homeowners in Vic. and SA suffered these traumas on 16 February 1983 - an infamous day known as Ash Wednesday.

For almost a year prior to that February Vic. had suffered its severest drought on record,

1980 Greg Norman wins his first Australian Golf Open

and Wednesday the 16th was another stifling day, reaching 43°C. The cocktail of soaring temperatures, strong winds, low humidity, and parched forests made for an extreme bush fire hazard. Throughout the day, for a number of reasons; trees touching power-lines, discarded cigarettes, and amazingly, deviants deliberately lighting them - bush fires flared. About 180 separate fires started and although most were under control by that night, 375,000 hectares of bush (an area the size of Luxembourg) was burnt off, 2,000 homes in Vic. and 100's in SA were destroyed, and 76 people had died.

Camping:
Lithgow Tourist & Van Park, 58 Cooerwull Rd, Lithgow, Ph (02) 6351 4350, T$10 ☐ Venice Caravan Park, Cnr Great Western Hwy & Gap Rd, Hartley, Ph (02) 6355 2106, T$7 ☐ Blackheath Caravan Park, Prince Edward St, Blackheath, Ph (02) 4787 8101, T$7 ☐ Katoomba Falls Park, Katoomba Falls Rd, Katoomba, Ph (02) 4782 1835, T$10

Hostel:
Blue Mountains YHA, 66 Waratah St, Katoomba, Ph (02) 4782 1416, Dm$20, D$55 ☐ Katoomba Mountain Lodge, 31 Lurline St, Katoomba, Ph (02) 4782 3933, Dm$15, D$42 ☐ Others; Katoomba

Motel/Hotel:
Lithgow Valley Inn, 45 Cooerwall Rd, Lithgow, Ph (02) 6351 2334, S$45, D$60 ☐ The Imperial Hotel, Great Western Hwy, Mt Victoria, Ph (02) 47 87 1878,
S$55, D$70 ☐ High Mountains Motel, 193 Great Western Hwy, Blackheath, Ph (02) 4787 8216, S$55, D$65 ☐ Colonial Motor Inn, 181 Great Western Hwy, Katoomba, Ph (02) 4782 1811, S$55, D$65 ☐ Three Sisters Motel, 348 Katoomba St (Cnr Katoomba & Birdwood Ave), Katoomba, Ph (02) 4782 2911, S$65, D$80 ☐ Others; Lithgow, Mt Victoria, Blackheath, Katoomba

i:
Lithgow Visitors Centre, Old Bowenfels Railway Stn, 1 Cooerwull Rd, Lithgow, Ph (02) 6353 1859 ☐ Blue Mountains Accommodation & Visitors Guide, Blackheath, Ph (02) 6355 6200 ☐ Katoomba Info. Centre, Echo Point Rd, Katoomba, Ph (02) 4739 6266

Bike Shop:
Cycletech, 182 Katoomba St, Katoomba, Ph (02) 4782 2800

4100km 30km before Lithgow

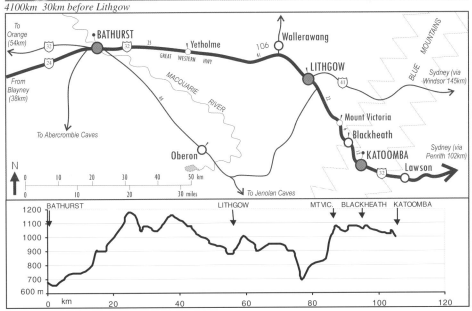

30 KATOOMBA TO BONDI BEACH

Katoomba to:

Penrith	53km	c, m/h, i, bike shop
Parramatta	82km	m/h, i, bike shop
Sydney City (Glebe)	102km	c, h, m/h, i, bike shop

Sydney City to:

Bondi Beach	9km	h, m/h, bike shop

The final leg of the journey drops off the Blue Mountains, crosses the Sydney Plain, and ends at Bondi Beach on the edge of the Pacific Ocean. Agreeably, this last section is mostly downhill or flat, however the traffic is heavy, frenetic, and unpredictable as the tour enters Australia's largest city.

The tentacles of Sydney's suburbs spread out in every direction along the roads into the city, with the longest arm creeping into the Blue Mountains almost to Katoomba. After Katoomba the highway passes through small towns with expensive homes nestled in the bush. As you descend, the Blue Mountains microclimate fades and the air warms.

At the foot of the mountains is a sign signalling the start of the M4 freeway to Sydney. Bikes are allowed on the wide smooth shoulder of the freeway all the way to Parramatta, where the M4 turns into a toll way and cyclists must turn-off. The freeway is the quickest way into the city and actually feels safe compared to the alternative; The Great Western Highway which has many traffic lights and vehicles close at your shoulder. After exiting the M4 at Parramatta continue with caution along the Great Western Highway (Route 32) which leads into central Sydney (an alternative is to take one of the river ferries from Parramatta right into downtown).

The Great Western Highway turns into Broadway and passes Sydney University in the suburb of Glebe - a good area to stay if you want to tackle the last 9km to Bondi fresh. Broadway joins George St near the Central Railway Station. George St is Sydney's main thoroughfare and leads through the central business district to Sydney Cove, the Harbour Bridge, and the Opera House.

To get to Bondi go right off George St onto Liverpool St about 1km past the Central Railway Station. Continue on Liverpool St until just past Hyde Park then veer right onto Oxford St, which eventually passes Centennial Park. About 1km past Centennial Park is Bondi Junction, take Bondi Rd down to the beach.

Bondi is Sydney's most famous beach. The name comes from an Aboriginal word meaning, "sound of the surf" and Australia's first lifesaving club was formed here in 1906.

Australia's Bicentennial

In 1988, Sydney celebrated its bicentennial with a big bash to mark 200 years of European settlement (although Aborigines had lived on the land for at least 50,000 years). The focus of the celebration was Sydney Cove, where the First Fleet set up camp on 21 January 1788. The 11 British Navy ships that sailed into Port Jackson were under the command of Captain Arthur Phillip, and had spent 8 months on the voyage from Portsmouth. 1,473 people were aboard - including 586 male prisoners and 192 female prisoners. They arrived at a place Cook had discovered only 18 years earlier.

The First Fleet was an experiment with the dual aims of colonising the continent and alleviating the overcrowding in London's prison system, which at the time included prisoners held in rotting Navy hulks anchored in the Thames River.

When Captain Phillip stepped ashore there were an estimated 750,000 Aborigines living on the land. Almost immediately the Aboriginal population started dropping as a result of introduced diseases and hostilities with the newcomers. After 45 years

1982 Lindy Chamberlain is convicted of murder despite her assertion that a dingo took her baby at Ayers Rock. In 1987 she is pardoned and in 1988 her conviction is quashed

European and Aboriginal numbers were about equal at 200,000 apiece, and it was not until the 1930's that the Aboriginal population started recovering. By 1988 Australia's population was 16,000,000 (250,000 of this number classed themselves as Aboriginal) and the country had moved from the Stone Age into the modern world. The bicentennial was marked by tall ships sailing into Sydney and a re-enactment of the January 1788 landing, and by Aboriginal rights protests - a pretty accurate summary of the situation.

(Note: For Sydney and Bondi details see p114)

Camping:
Penrith Caravan Park, MacKellar St, Emu Plains, Ph (02) 4735 4425, T$10 Others; Emu Plains (2km W of Penrith)

Motel/Hotel:
Pioneer Way Motel, 429 Great Western Hwy, Faulconbridge (30km E of Katoomba), Ph (02) 4751 2194, S$60, D$75 ▯ Penrith Valley Inn, Great Western Hwy, Penrith, Ph (02) 4731 1666, S$115, D$130 ▯ Parramatta City Motel, Great Western Hwy, Parramatta, Ph (02) 9635 7266, S$92, D$97 ▯ Others; Penrith, Parramatta

i:
Penrith Information Centre, Mulgoa Rd, Penrith, Ph (02) 4732 7671 ▯ Parramatta Visitors Information Centre, 346 Church St, Parramatta, Ph (02) 9630 3703

Bike Shops:
Blue Mountains Cycles, Shop 2, 4 Raymond Rd, Springwood, Ph (02) 4751 1601 ▯ Blaxland Bicycles, 3 Station St, Blaxland (41km E of Katoomba), Ph (02) 4739 3166 ▯ Blackman Bicycles, Edwards Pl, Penrith, Ph (02) 4731 3048 ▯ The Bike Barn, 382 Church St, Parramatta, Ph (02) 9630 3844 ▯ Others; Penrith, Parramatta

4200km Near Woodford in the Blue Mountains

4300km 2km before Bondi Beach

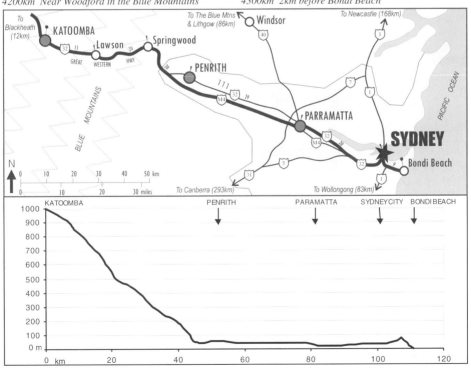

1982 Paul Caffyn, a New Zealander, circumnavigates Australia by kayak. The trip takes over a year

113

SYDNEY

The biggest and brashest city in Australia was also the first to be settled. In January 1788, the First Fleet sailed into **Port Jackson** and set up camp at **Sydney Cove**. An urban sprawl of nearly four million has grown up around this little cove, which is still the heart of Sydney and the best place from which to start an exploration of the city.

At the head of Sydney Cove is **Circular Quay**, where **Harbour cruises** and **ferries** to the **North Shore** beaches and **Parramatta** depart. The Cove is flanked by the dual icons of **Sydney Opera House** (the city's bickering with the Danish architect, who left mid-construction, all but forgotten now) and **Sydney Harbour Bridge**. On the west side of the bay is **The Rocks**, the site of Sydney's first raucous settlement and the location of many executions in those early days. The area is now a mix of preserved buildings and swank shops and restaurants. Above The Rocks is **Observatory Hill**, the highest point in the city and the location for **Sydney Observatory**. The city's lights dull the telescope but on clear nights you can view Jupiter's spot (on cloudy nights you get to see the Balmian clock tower instead).

Government House and the **Royal Botanic Gardens** are on the east side of the cove. The 1843 gothic revival Government House was the Governor of New South Wales's residence until 1996 when the Government gave it back to the city and it was opened to the public. The Botanic Gardens wrap around the foreshore into Farm Cove - the site of the settlements first attempts at agriculture, which, partly due to the poor soil, had the colony on the verge of starvation until the Second Fleet arrived two years later. At the eastern tip of Farm Cove is **Mrs Macquaries Chair**, the 1810 Governor's wife's favourite lookout.

The city's **civic centre** extends inland from Sydney Cove. The main thoroughfare is **George St** with the **General Post Office**, **Town Hall,** and the **Cenotaph**. A popular shopping spot is the restored **Queen Victoria Building**. **Sydney Tower**, the tallest structure in the city, is on Market St and includes a lookout deck and revolving restaurant.

Sydney has a stack of other interesting sites and historical landmarks; try a walk round **Darling Harbour**, the hands-on **Powerhouse Museum** or the trendy cafes of **Glebe**, or stroll along Macquarie St past the **Conservatorium of Music** (designed by the convict architect Francis Greenway as Governor Macquarie's stables), the **NSW State Library**, the **Mint Museum**, and **Hyde Park Barracks** (an excellent museum).

Possibilities for trips outside the city include the pretty **North** and **South Coast** areas.

Camping:
Lane Cove Caravan Park, Plassey Rd, North Ryde, Ph (02) 9888 9133, T$17 (10km NW of downtown) ☐ Sheralee Caravan Park, 88 Bryant St, Rockdale, Ph (02) 9567 7161, T$12 (13km S of downtown) ☐ La Manch Cara Park, 901 Pacific Hwy, Berowra, Ph (02) 9456 1766, T$23 (30km NW of downtown)

Hostel:
Nomads Forest Lodge, 117 Arundel St, Glebe, Ph (02) 9660 1872, Dm$15, D$50 ☐ Glebe Village Backpackers, 256 Glebe Pt Rd, Glebe, Ph (02) 9660 8133, Dm$21, S$60, D$60 ☐ Central Sydney YHA, 11 Rawson Pl, Sydney, Ph (02) 9281 9111, Dm$25, D$70 ☐ Backpackers Planet, 198 Elizabeth St, Sydney, Ph (02) 9211 7371, Dm$30 ☐ Indy's Beachside Backpackers, 35A Hall St, Bondi, Ph (02) 9365 4900, Dm$21, S$50, D$50 ☐ Others; Sydney

Motel/Hotel:
The Glebe Motel, 196 Glebe Pt Rd, Glebe, Ph (02) 9660 6655, S$110, D$110 ☐ University Motor Inn, 25 Arundel St, Glebe, Ph (02) 9660 5777, S$137, D$141 ☐ Park Regis Motel, 27 Park St, Sydney, Ph (02) 9267 6511, S$130, D$130 ☐ The Castlereagh Inn, 169 Castlereagh St, Sydney, Ph (02) 9284 1000, S$127, D$127 ☐ Alice Motel, 30 Fletcher St, Bondi Beach, Ph (02) 9130 5231, S$75, D$85 ☐ Bondi Beachside Inn, 152 Campbell Pde, Bondi Beach, Ph (02) 9130 5311, S$90, D$90 ☐ Others; Sydney

i:
Sydney Visitor Centre, Martin Pl, Sydney, Ph (02) 9235 2424 ☐ Sydney Visitor Centre, 106 George St, Sydney, Ph (02) 9255 1788

Bike Shops:
Inner City Cycles, 151 Glebe Pt Rd, Glebe, Ph (02) 9660 6605 ☐ Bicycles in the City, 722 George St, Sydney, Ph (02) 9280 2229 ☐ Bondi Junction Cycles, 310 Oxford St, Bondi Junction, Ph (02) 9369 4443 ☐ Others; Sydney

1983 The Fremantle Yacht Club wins the America's Cup assisted by a revolutionary winged keel

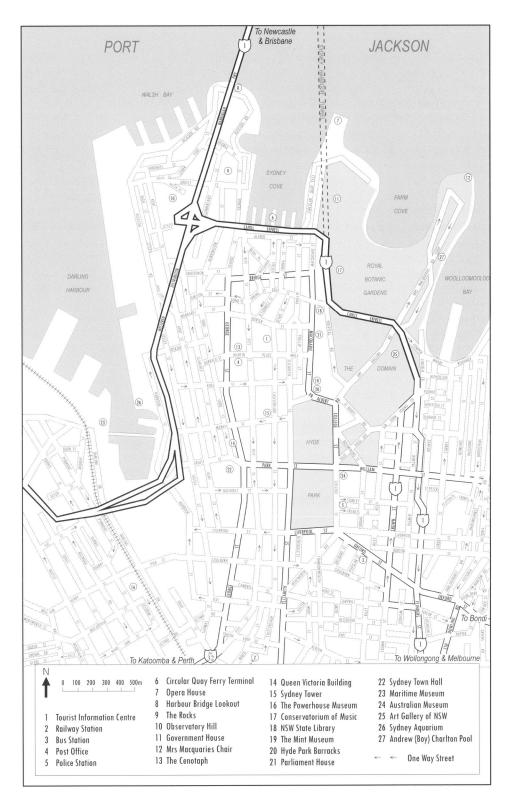

PORT

JACKSON

WALSH BAY

SYDNEY
COVE

FARM
COVE

DARLING
HARBOUR

ROYAL
BOTANIC
GARDENS

WOOLLOOMOOLOO
BAY

THE
DOMAIN

HYDE

PARK

PARK

To Newcastle
& Brisbane

To Katoomba & Perth

To Wollongong & Melbourne

To Bondi

N

0 100 200 300 400 500m

1 Tourist Information Centre
2 Railway Station
3 Bus Station
4 Post Office
5 Police Station

6 Circular Quay Ferry Terminal
7 Opera House
8 Harbour Bridge Lookout
9 The Rocks
10 Observatory Hill
11 Government House
12 Mrs Macquaries Chair
13 The Cenotaph

14 Queen Victoria Building
15 Sydney Tower
16 The Powerhouse Museum
17 Conservatorium of Music
18 NSW State Library
19 The Mint Museum
20 Hyde Park Barracks
21 Parliament House

22 Sydney Town Hall
23 Maritime Museum
24 Australian Museum
25 Art Gallery of NSW
26 Sydney Aquarium
27 Andrew (Boy) Charlton Pool

← ← One Way Street

4302km The end of the road, Bondi Beach

1984 "God Save the Queen" is replaced by "Advance Australia Fair" as the national anthem

ALTERNATIVE: AROUND TASMAINIA

Tasmania, or "Tassi", has a justifiably clean green image. With a wetter climate than the mainland, it is forested, mountainous, and 25% of the total area is National Park land. A cycle tour around Tasmania involves considerable climbing but this is rewarded with beautiful scenery. You can fly to Tasmania, or take the daily ferry from Melbourne to Devonport on the north coast. An anticlockwise tour around the island, starting at Devonport, would follow the coastal cliffs to Somerset then head inland through farmland to the rugged Western Ranges. The road passes through the barren tin and copper mining areas around Queenstown then through the Cradle Mountain-Lake St. Claire National Park (a great place for hiking). This part of the island is so rugged that it was 1932 before a road was finally pushed through. Every few years a local in one of these remote areas will report seeing a Tasmanian Tiger, the largest of the carnivorous marsupials, and a species presumed extinct after the last animal died in a Tasmanian zoo in 1936. From the highlands the route drops through pretty farmland to the state capital Hobart, the second oldest city in Australia, then crosses the Derwent River via Tasman Bridge (a freighter struck this bridge in 1975, demolishing the centre span and killing 13 people). The road up the east coast passes picturesque seaside towns before climbing inland over hilly country to the major town of Launceston. A possible Tasmanian tour could be:

Devonport to Henrietta (85km) ☐ Henrietta to Tullah (78km) ☐ Tullah to Queenstown (68km) ☐ Queenstown to Derwent Bridge (81km) ☐ Derwent Bridge to Ouse (85km) ☐ Ouse to Hobart (88km) ☐ Hobart to Triabunna (88km) ☐ Triabunna to Bicheno (94km) ☐ Bicheno to St Helens (83km) ☐ St Helens to Branxholm (76km) ☐ Branxholm to Launceston (94km) ☐ Launceston to Devonport (101km)

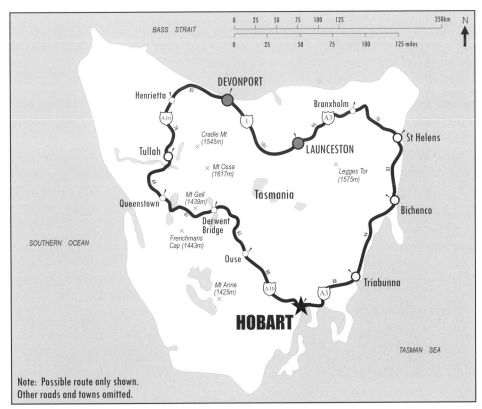

Note: Possible route only shown.
Other roads and towns omitted.

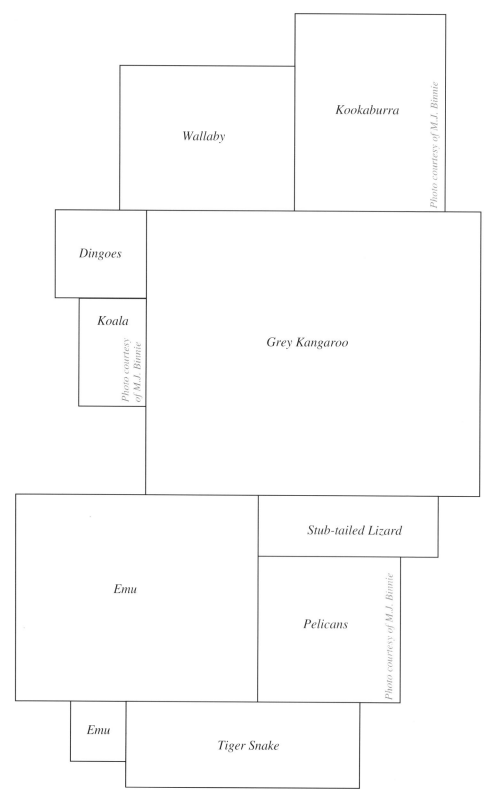

Wallaby

Kookaburra

Photo courtesy of M.J. Binnie

Dingoes

Koala

Photo courtesy of M.J. Binnie

Grey Kangaroo

Stub-tailed Lizard

Emu

Pelicans

Photo courtesy of M.J. Binnie

Emu

Tiger Snake

1987 Australia loses the America's Cup back to the Americans

1987 Midnight Oil, a band of high school mates which started
      out playing Sydney's surf beaches, releases "Diesel and
      Dust", the biggest selling album in Australian recording history

1988 Bicentennial celebrations mark 200 years of European settlement

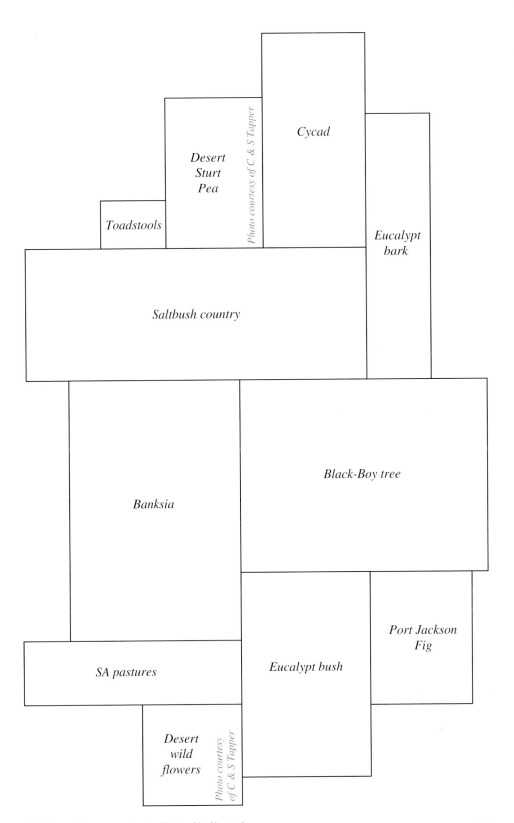

Cycad

Desert
Sturt
Pea

Photo courtesy of C & S Tapper

Toadstools

Eucalypt
bark

Saltbush country

Black-Boy tree

Banksia

SA pastures

Eucalypt bush

Port Jackson
Fig

Desert
wild
flowers

Photo courtesy
of C & S Tapper

APPENDIX A: TEMPERATURE & RAINFALL

PERTH

	Av. Min (°C)	Av. Max (°C)	Min (°C)	Max (°C)	Rain (days)	Rain (mm)
Jan	17	32	6	46	2	10
Feb	18	32	6	47	3	15
Mar	16	30	5	43	4	15
Apr	13	25	1	38	7	40
May	10	22	0	34	13	105
Jun	9	18	-1	28	17	175
Jul	8	17	-1	26	18	160
Aug	8	18	0	28	16	120
Sep	9	20	0	32	14	70
Oct	10	23	3	38	10	45
Nov	13	25	3	41	7	25
Dec	15	29	5	42	4	15

NORSEMAN

	Av. Min (°C)	Av. Max (°C)	Min (°C)	Max (°C)	Rain (days)	Rain (mm)
Jan	15	33	6	46	3	17
Feb	15	31	6	45	4	24
Mar	14	29	4	44	5	23
Apr	12	24	0	37	5	23
May	8	20	-2	33	7	31
Jun	6	17	-3	28	8	32
Jul	5	16	-3	28	9	27
Aug	6	18	-2	30	8	25
Sep	8	22	-2	35	7	21
Oct	10	15	-1	40	5	20
Nov	12	28	2	41	4	20
Dec	14	31	3	45	4	21

EUCLA

	Av. Min (°C)	Av. Max (°C)	Min (°C)	Max (°C)	Rain (days)	Rain (mm)
Jan	16	26	3	48	3	13
Feb	16	26	8	47	4	18
Mar	15	25	7	45	6	21
Apr	13	23	2	40	8	26
May	10	21	0	36	10	32
Jun	8	18	0	33	10	29
Jul	7	18	-1	28	10	25
Aug	8	19	0	33	9	26
Sep	9	21	0	40	8	21
Oct	11	23	3	43	6	19
Nov	13	24	4	44	5	17
Dec	15	25	7	45	4	17

CEDUNA

	Av. Min (°C)	Av. Max (°C)	Min (°C)	Max (°C)	Rain (days)	Rain (mm)
Jan	15	29	5	48	3	12
Feb	15	29	5	47	3	14
Mar	13	27	1	46	4	16
Apr	10	24	2	40	7	20
May	8	21	-3	34	10	35
Jun	7	18	-5	30	11	36
Jul	6	17	-4	32	13	42
Aug	6	18	-3	32	12	35
Sep	8	21	-2	40	10	28
Oct	10	23	0	43	8	26
Nov	12	26	2	46	6	21
Dec	13	27	3	47	5	21

ADELAIDE

	Av. Min (°C)	Av. Max (°C)	Min (°C)	Max (°C)	Rain (days)	Rain (mm)
Jan	15	28	8	44	5	17
Feb	15	28	8	43	4	25
Mar	14	25	4	41	6	18
Apr	12	22	3	37	9	44
May	9	18	0	30	13	66
Jun	8	16	-3	25	14	52
Jul	6	14	-1	26	16	60
Aug	7	16	0	27	16	48
Sep	8	18	1	34	13	42
Oct	10	21	3	38	11	34
Nov	12	23	4	42	8	29
Dec	14	26	5	42	7	24

MILDURA

	Av. Min (°C)	Av. Max (°C)	Min (°C)	Max (°C)	Rain (days)	Rain (mm)
Jan	17	32	8	48	4	22
Feb	16	31	5	45	3	20
Mar	13	28	4	42	4	19
Apr	10	23	2	38	5	19
May	8	19	-1	30	7	28
Jun	5	16	-3	25	8	23
Jul	4	15	-4	27	9	27
Aug	5	17	-2	30	9	27
Sep	7	20	-1	36	8	29
Oct	10	24	1	40	7	32
Nov	12	28	3	45	7	24
Dec	14	30	5	46	5	22

BALRANALD

	Av. Min (°C)	Av. Max (°C)	Min (°C)	Max (°C)	Rain (days)	Rain (mm)
Jan	16	33	8	48	3	22
Feb	16	33	7	47	3	23
Mar	13	30	1	43	3	22
Apr	10	23	2	38	4	23
May	7	19	-3	36	6	33
Jun	4	16	-4	25	7	30
Jul	3	15	-5	27	8	26
Aug	5	18	-3	30	7	30
Sep	8	21	-2	36	6	30
Oct	10	25	-4	41	5	32
Nov	12	28	3	43	5	26
Dec	15	31	5	46	4	25

SYDNEY

	Av. Min (°C)	Av. Max (°C)	Min (°C)	Max (°C)	Rain (days)	Rain (mm)
Jan	18	26	10	45	12	104
Feb	18	25	10	43	12	117
Mar	17	24	9	40	14	130
Apr	14	22	7	33	12	128
May	12	20	4	30	12	121
Jun	9	17	2	27	11	130
Jul	8	16	2	26	10	98
Aug	9	18	3	32	10	82
Sep	11	20	5	35	10	70
Oct	13	22	6	38	11	75
Nov	15	23	8	42	11	82
Dec	18	25	9	43	12	78

1991 Bob Hawke; Rhode Scholar, ex-national drinking champion, and Australia's longest serving Prime Minister loses office

APPENDIX B: ADDITIONAL INFORMATION

Books:

Field Guide to the Birds of Australia. Ken Simpson & Nicolas Day. Penguin Books Australia 1999. *Detailed sketches make this a standard for bird identification in Australia.*

A Photographic Guide to Mammals of Australia. Ronald Straham. New Holland 1995. *Excellent photos in a slimline book.*

Reading the Rocks. Mary E. White. Kangaroo Press 1999. *Explores the paleo-environments of Australia and New Zealand.*

Reptiles and Amphibians of Australia. Harold G. Cogger. Reed New Holland 2000. *A thick book with lots of species distribution maps and good photos.*

Archaeology of Aboriginal Australia. Ed. Tim Murray. Allen & Unwin 1998. *Papers from the last 30 years of Australian archaeology.*

Archaeology of the Dreamtime; The Story of Prehistoric Australia and its People. Josephine Flood. 1995. *Scholarly but interesting.*

The Australians. The Way We Live Now. Ross Terrill. Doubleday 2000. *The present pulse of the country.*

Feet of Clay. Fiona Campbell. 1994. *An account of one woman's walk across Australia. Her route in SA and WA follows much of the route in this guide.*

The Bicycle and the Bush. Man and Machine in Rural Australia. Jim Fitzpatrick. Oxford University Press 1980. *A great read on the use of bicycles in early Aust.*

Australia Twice Traversed Vol. 1 & 2. Ernest Giles. *An Englishman's account of his 5 expeditions, between 1872 and 1876, through SA, NT, and WA.*

Walking the Simpson Desert. C. Warren Bonython. *You think cycling Australia is tough? Read this.*

Movies:

Walkabout. 1971. *Moves from the city to the Outback and examines the Aboriginal/European culture clash.*

Mad Max. 1979. *This bloody Aussie movie was Mel Gibson's breakout role and is a cult classic.*

The Castle. 1997. *Comedy about a Melbourne family's fight to prevent their house being taken for a runway extension. Biggest grossing film in Aust. in 1997.*

Shine. 1996. *Virtuoso pianist David Helfgott's troubled childhood, psychiatric problems, and tortured genius.*

Proof. 1992. *Interesting movie about a blind man who likes taking photos, co-stars Russell Crowe.*

Gallipoli. 1981. *The story of two young Australians at this fruitless and fateful WWI assault in Turkey.*

Strictly Ballroom. 1992. *Basic love story injected with laconic Australian humor.*

A Cry in the Dark (Australian Title: Evil Angels). 1988. *Recounts the disappearance of baby Azaria Chamberlain at Ayers Rock, the mother's claim that a dingo took the baby, and the subsequent murder trial.*

Internet sites:

www.pm.gov.au *The Australian Prime Minister's web site.*

www.aa.gov.au *The National Archives of Australia.*

www.csu.edu.au *An entry point for an on-line encyclopedia of Australia, hosted by Charles Sturt University.*

www.tourism.wa.gov.au
www.tourism.sa.gov.au
www.tourism.vic.gov.au
www.tourism.nsw.gov.au *State tourism commission web sites for WA,, SA, Vic., and NSW.*

www.csiro.au *Australia's largest scientific research agency has its web pages here.*

www.agso.gov.au *The Australian Geological Survey.*

www.bfa.asn.au *Links to the Bicycle Federation of Australia, the national body for bicycle advocacy.*

Newspapers, Magazines and Periodicals:

The Bulletin. *Australia's equivalent of Time magazine, but better.*

The Sydney Morning Herald and The Melbourne Age. *The two largest non-tabloid daily papers.*

Geo. *An excellent monthly publication from the Australian Geographic Society.*

Australian Bicycling. *A monthly magazine that includes road and mountain bike news and articles.*

Pop Music:

Little River Band. *One of the first Australian bands to hit it big internationally.*

Men at Work. *Melbourne band that formed in 1979. "Down Under" was their huge hit. Recently reformed.*

Cold Chisel. *Quintessential 80's Aussie rock.*

Hoodo Gurus. *Semi-alternative 80's band with hits like "What's My Scene" and "1000 Miles Away".*

INXS *Sold 20 million records over 20 years before the suicide of front man Michael Hutchence.*

Midnight Oil. *Australian power rockers for the last 25 years, lead by Peter Garrett. Their music includes strong stands on environmental and aboriginal issues.*

Silverchair. *One of the biggest bands out of Australia in the 1990's. A three piece hard rock group.*

1992 The Mabo Treaty is ratified, refuting the previously held position that Australia was not owned by anyone prior to European settlement

123

APPENDIX C: METRIC CONVERSIONS

TEMPERATURE

To convert °C to °F multiply by 1.8 and add 32
To convert °F to °C subtract 32 and multiply by 0.555

°C	=	°F		°F	=	°C
50		122		120		49
45		113		110		43
40		104		100		38
35		95		90		32
30		86		80		27
25		77		70		21
20		68		60		16
15		59		50		10
10		50		40		4
5		41		30		-1
0		32		20		-7
-5		23		10		-12
-10		14		0		-18
-15		5		-10		-23

DISTANCE

To convert kilometres to miles multiply by 0.621
To convert miles to kilometres multiply by 1.61

km	=	miles		miles	=	km
1		0.621		1		1.61
2		1.2		2		3.2
3		1.9		3		4.8
4		2.5		4		6.4
5		3.1		5		8.1
6		3.7		6		9.7
7		4.4		7		11.3
8		5.0		8		12.9
9		5.6		9		14.5
10		6.2		10		16.1

To convert metres to feet multiply by 3.28
To convert feet to meters multiply by 0.305

m	=	ft		ft	=	m
1		3.28		1		0.305
2		6.6		2		0.6
3		9.8		3		0.9
4		13.1		4		1.2
5		16.4		5		1.5
6		19.7		6		1.8
7		23.0		7		2.1
8		26.2		8		2.4
9		29.5		9		2.8
10		32.8		10		3.1

(To convert metres to yards multiply by 0.91. To convert yards to metres multiply by 1.09)
(To convert km^2 into $miles^2$ multiply by 0.39. To convert $mile^2$ into km^2 multiply by 2.59)
(To convert cm to inches multiply by 0.39. To convert inches to cm multiply by 2.54)
(There are 10mm in a cm, and 100cm in a m)

1996 The Prime Minister, Paul Keating, is dubbed "The
Lizard of Oz" by the British Press after putting his arm
around Queen Elizabeth during a Royal visit

WEIGHT

To convert kilograms to pounds multiply by 2.20
To convert pounds to kilograms multiply by 0.455

kg	=	lbs		lbs	=	kg
1		2.20		1		0.455
2		4.4		2		0.9
3		6.6		3		1.4
4		8.8		4		1.8
5		11.0		5		2.3
6		13.2		6		2.7
7		15.4		7		3.2
8		17.6		8		3.6
9		19.8		9		4.1
10		22.0		10		4.6

To convert grams to ounces multiply by 0.35
To convert ounces to grams multiply by 28.4

g	=	oz		oz	=	g
1		0.35		1		28.4
2		0.7		2		57
3		1.1		3		85
4		1.4		4		114
5		1.8		5		142
6		2.1		6		170
7		2.5		7		199
8		2.8		8		227
9		3.2		9		256
10		3.5		10		284

1 British ton = 1019kg (2240lbs)
1 US ton = 910kg (2000lbs)
(To convert British tons to US tons multiply by 0.893)

VOLUME

To convert litres to US gallons multiply by 0.264
To convert US gallons to litres multiply by 3.79

litre	=	US gal		US gal	=	litre
1		0.264		1		3.79
2		0.5		2		7.6
3		0.8		3		11.4
4		1.1		4		15.1
5		1.3		5		19.0
6		1.6		6		22.7
7		1.8		7		26.5
8		2.1		8		30.3
9		2.4		9		34.1
10		2.6		10		37.9

(1 litre is 1.5 US pints, and 1.8 UK pints)
(1 imperial gallon = 4.55 liters (1.18 US gallons))
(To convert US gallons to imperial gallons multiply by 0.845)
(1 cubic meter = 35.3 cubic feet, 1 cubic foot = 0.0283 cubic meters)
(1 Acre = 0.4047 hectares, 1 hectare = 2.47 acres)

INDEX

2000 Sydney Harbour Bridge is closed for a morning as Aboriginal rights protestors march across during national Reconciliation Week.

About the Author

Born and raised in New Zealand, Paul developed a passion for cycle touring while studying geology at Auckland University. He cycled solo across Australia after an end to end trip of New Zealand. Since then he has completed trips in several other countries. Paul is married to Eileen and currently works as a geologist in California.

www.epicguides.co.nz

QUESTIONNAIRE

This guide was developed to provide the information you need for an epic cycling trip across Australia. We'd like get your feedback, and welcome any suggestions you might have.

We'd also like to hear about your trip; the high- and low-points, and any comments you have about the route, accommodation, or services along the way. Completing this questionnaire will lighten your load!

How did you hear about this guide?
Bookshop (which one?)................. ☐		Friends................. ☐
Bike Shop (which one?)................. ☐		Internet................. ☐
Other...

Where did you get "Bike Australia"?
Bookshop (which one?)................. ☐		Gift...................... ☐
Bike Shop (which one?)................. ☐		Internet................. ☐
Other...

Which parts of the guide did you find most useful?......................................
....

What would you like to see included in the next edition of this guide?..................
....

What other countries would you like to see Epic Cycling Guides for?....................
....

Comments...
....
....

Two more Epic Guides are due out soon. Would you like further information on these guides?

Bike New Zealand, Cycling NZ
from Cape Reinga to Bluff............... ☐

Bike Britain, Cycling From Land's
End to John o' Groats................. ☐

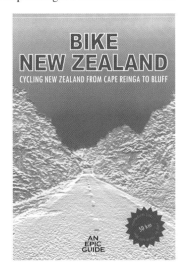

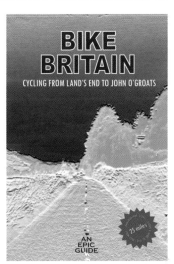

Name:....................................... Address:..
.... E-mail:..

Post to: Epic Guides, P.O. Box 31053, Milford, New Zealand